BRAIN GAMES
from
Walter Joris

MORE FROM TARQUIN
Tarquin has hundreds of mathematical books, posters and games
for all ages on our website www.tarquingroup.com

© 2024: Walter Joris

ISBN: 978-1-913565-35-0
Ebook 978-1-858118-52-1

Design: Julie Peasley, PointLinePlane
Printing: Printed in the UK and USA

Tarquin
Suite 74, 17 Holywell Hill
St Albans AL1 1DT
United Kingdom

www.tarquingroup.com

About the Author

Walter Joris is a Belgian author. He has had two TV series in the Netherlands plus some comedy on Belgian (Flemish) TV. He wrote and published humorous books in Dutch and made a living as a standup comedian in the Netherlands and Belgium. He is the author of *100 Strategic Games in Pen and Paper*, which was written in English and translated into several languages. Walter has had several exhibitions with all kinds of artwork.

He lives by the sea in Belgium.

WELCOME

We are delighted to introduce this collection of games that are both fun and designed to engage your brain. Many are designed to be played with friends or family, and just as many by yourself.

Brain Games are not for younger children, but enjoying them is not restricted to any particular age group. Many adults will love them as much as we have producing the book. Using Walter's quirky and amusing drawings, games are quick to learn and many can be played for hours.

Games include:
- Number games for 1 and 2 players
- Logic games for 1 and 2 players
- Drawing games
- Action games
- Paper engineering games
- Word games

If you want to do a particular type of game, look out for the icons on page 7 as you go through. Or play the 239 Games in order and challenge yourself and your skills!

Walter Joris has been amusing and challenging people for many years – see more about Walter on the last page of the book.

Tarquin

The Games

KEY TO ICONS

 SOLO GAME

 2-PERSON GAME

 PAPER ENGINEERING

 DRAWING GAME

 WORD GAME

 ACTION GAME

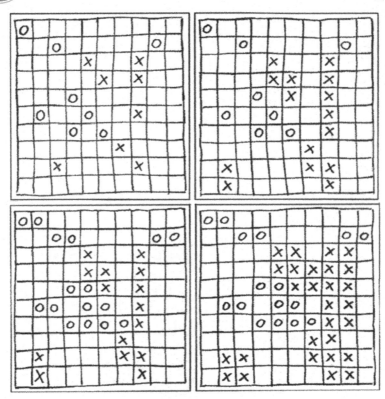

PLAY ON A 10X10 GRID. Players take turns to draw a total of 8 of their own marks (circle or cross) somewhere on the board. After that, with each move, each player chooses a direction: up, down, left, or right.

If, for example, Cross chooses down, then he moves his whole group of crosses one square downwards. This means that under each cross he can put one extra (if that square is free). Then it's the opponent's turn. Each time the direction is freely chosen. Whoever can't play anymore has to pass, and let the other play on. The winner is the one with the most marks.

EXAMPLES

1. Situation after 8 marks.
2. First stampede of Cross downwards.
3. Stampede of Circle to the right.
4. Also Cross does a stampede to the right.

THREEBLOCK

A →

1	2	3
1	3	3
2	2	1

1	1	3
1	2	3
3	3	3

19
22

B↓ C↘

1	3	1			
2	3	2		6	
2	1	3			6

2	2	3	6	5	6
2	1	1	5	4	5
1	2	2	✕	5	5

DRAW, FREEHAND, A BOARD LIKE THIS. In turn blue and red (or, like here, blank and dot) place 3 separate 1s, 2s, and 3s in the 3 x 3 blocks A and B, anywhere they want. After that, they may add up one digit from A, plus one from B, and write the sum in square C. But only where the row and the column from A and B meet. See example: dot places a 6, and blank also. This is done in turn. One square will be left open.

Winner is the one with the highest total. In the example, it is blank.

3 DIGIMORPH

67213	39876	678241	739843	739843
61021	91587	714241	109843	73987
6301	91515	84241	10 8412	73816
640	97101	42121	104110	73114
10	10101	6121		3814
		721		817
		91		115
		10		

WRITE DOWN A RANDOM NUMBER. Then add up two chosen digits. Go on until you reach all zeros and ones.

This can also be played as a game for two, each departing from the same number. Mistakes however may not be corrected. When you don't reach all zeros and ones, the number containing the nearest number to 1 wins. See example on the right: the number 4 is the lowest and wins.

TUMBLEBLOCK

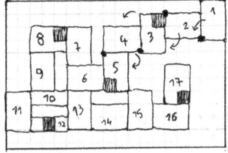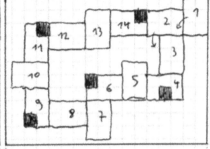

PASTIME SOLO GAME. On squared paper draw an 18 x12 rectangle. Next, randomly, make 5 squares black. In the right corner draw a 3 by 2 block. Now turn this block along one of its 4 corners (only 90°). (First 4 pivot points and directions are indicated.)

Goal is to cover all 5 black squares in a minimum number of turns. It is allowed to turn over a previous position (as in 12). Here we did it in 17 turns. Is it possible to do this faster? Yes! See example 2. (Someone has shown me an even faster method.)

LINE CHAIR

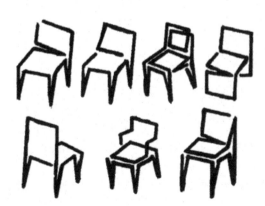

ART GAME AND PUZZLE.

Try to draw a series of chairs in one continuous line. To play with friends, each player has 5 minutes to invent as many of these as possible.

6 TENTANGLE

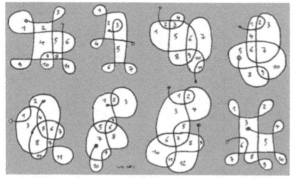

PASTIME DOODLE GAME. Try to draw exactly 10 closed spaces in one continuous line, without counting. This can be challenging, when using only your "subconscious counting." So I even made a painting from it!

7 PILEDIE

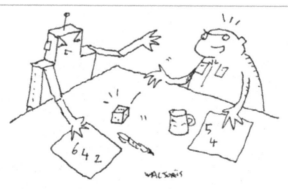

EACH PLAYER THROWS THE DIE in turn, having chosen a limited number of turns, for example 15. You can choose freely if you accept the number shown or reject it. If you accept, you must write it down. The goal is to achieve the highest "pile" of numbers, running from high to low. In the drawing, the left player wins: 3 numbers.

TACTICS: if you got a 6 or a 5 you better accept that number. There is still plenty of chance to collect lower numbers. But if you got a 6 followed by a 1, it's best to reject the 1, or you will end up with a pile of only two numbers. If the two piles are equal, the higher sum wins.

DOTSPRINKLER

Grid A

		3	x	1	•
	2	x	x	x	2
	•	•		•	x
•	•	1	•	3	•
•	4	x		x	4
	•			x	x

Grid B

		•	•	x	x	x
x	x	1	•	2	x	
x	3	x	4	x	x	
x	•	4	1	•	•	
•	2	x	•	3	•	
•	•	•	•	•	•	

Grid C

		4	x	2	
			x		

WE PLAY ON A 6 BY 6 GRID.

In turn blue and red each write a 1, 2, 3, 4. Here we use digits in white or grey squares, with dots for White and crosses for Grey. After that, you can draw, in turns, your marks (dots or crosses) somewhere in the 8 surrounding squares of your digit. A one gives one dot, a two, two dots, and so on. We start from 1 to 4. When that is finished, we start again from 1 to 4, until it becomes impossible. If one player is blocked, he has to pass his turn. The winner is the one with the most marks.

EXAMPLES

A. The game after the first 1 to 4.

B. A finished game: dot player wins (15 dots – 12 crosses).

C. It is of course strategically important to block your opponent. Therefore Grey 2 places his crosses in the possible space of 4.

⑨

ONE TEMPLATE CAR

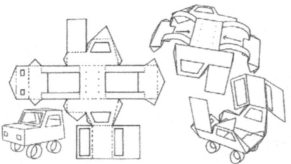

TRY TO DESIGN CARS

and other objects out of only ONE coherent template. Draw it freehand, this gives a more lively and artistic effect. It's a puzzle and a challenge in spatial thinking.

10 SEQUENCIUM

Grid A

1			6	7	8
	2	5	4	5	6
	4	3	4	7	
			3		
				2	
					1

Grid B

1			6	7	8
	2	5	4	5	6
		4	3	4	7
		5	5	3	8
	6		6	2	9
	7	9	8	7	1

Grid C

1	8	7	6	7	8
3	2	5	4	5	6
11	4	3	4	7	
10	5	5	3	8	
9	6	10	6	2	9
8	7	9	8	7	1

WE PLAY ON SQUARED PAPER,
6 by 6, in two colors (here grey and blank). Grey 1 starts at the top left corner, and blank 1 at the bottom right corner. From then on they may move to a higher number, straight or diagonal. It is permissible to count more than once from any lower number. The player who reaches the highest number wins.

EXAMPLES. A. Grey played from his 4 again (underlined) in order to block 5 to go downwards, to a lot of free space. On top 8 is blocked, but he can continue from his lower 4: 3, 2, 1 ... B. Blank escapes with a new number 5 (underlined). But when he jumped to 6, grey blocked him with 8 (underlined). Then again 7 (underlined), grey 9, blank 8, grey 6 and 7 (to block further expansion of this blank 9). C. Blank starts top row from 6 again (underlined): to the left: 7, 8. Blocked by grey 3. Grey Plays on from his 7, and reaches 11 and wins.

11 TRICYCLE

First row of squares

4 7 6	7 0 9	0 0 2	0 0 5	0 0 8	0 0 1	0 0 4	0 0 7	0 0 0	0 0 0
3 2 1	6 5 4	9 8 7	2 1 0	5 4 0	8 7 0	1 0 0	4 0 0	7 0 0	0 0 0
9 8 5	2 1 8	5 4 1	8 7 4	1 0 7	4 0 0	7 0 0	0 0 0	0 0 0	0 0 0

Second row of squares

4 7 6	1 4 3	8 1 0	5 8 0	2 5 0	3 2 0	6 9 0	3 6 0	0 3 0	0 0 0
3 2 1	0 9 8	0 6 5	0 3 2	0 0 9	0 0 6	0 0 3	0 0 0	0 0 0	0 0 0
9 8 5	6 5 2	3 2 9	0 9 6	0 6 3	0 3 0	0 0 0	0 0 0	0 0 0	0 0 0

NUMBER AMUSEMENT. Write down random digits in a 3 by 3 square. Then we add 3 to each digit. When we go over ten, the ten falls away. So for instance 9 + 3 = 2, not 12. Or 2 - 3 = 9. We go on until we reach zero (= 10) for each number. In the first row we added 3 to each digit. In the second row we subtracted 3 consistently. This also becomes zero for every number, in the end. Will this be possible with every number ? No: when we add with 4 instead of 3, we never reach zero. For instance: 3 + 4 = 7-1-5-9-3-7. But are there other possible numbers? This little pastime can also be done in many variations.

THE DOUBLE CUBE PUZZLE

1.	1	6
5	2	2.
5.	3	3.
4.	4	6.

USING TEMPLATE A, HOW DO YOU MAKE A 'DOUBLE SIDED' CUBE?
Solution: the numbers without a dot are the inner cube. Make that first.
(All dashed lines need to be creased; all solid lines must be cut.)
You can also cut a small window in the outer surface.

Next: try a "triple' cube with a template of 3 x 6...FUN!

 ## WRIGGLEFINGER

GAMES THAT WILL DRIVE YOU CRAZY. Weave a short rope through your fingers like this. Then try to wriggle it to the left until you reach the end. Once you mastered that, try it between your toes, on two feet simultaneously, in bed, in the dark…

SUBTERRANEAN LAIR

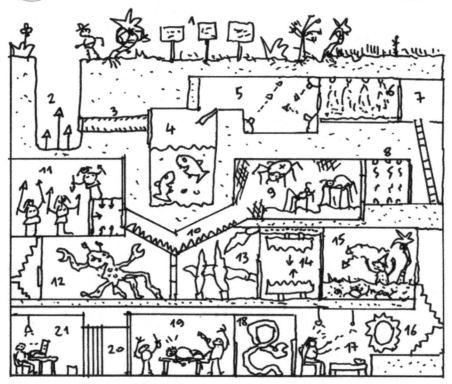

FANTASY GAME – GUESS THESE AND THEN DRAW YOUR OWN.

My example: 1. Warning signs. Invent a few funny ones. 2. Pit with spears. 3. Narrow crawl space with pins. 4. Water basin with sharks. 5. Robot machine guns. 6. Acid sprayers. 7. Old ladder missing a few steps. 8. Radioactive plutonium room. 9. Giant spiders. 10. Narrow passage with poisonous barbs. 11. Amazon Warrior Women throwing spears at you. 12. Alien from the planet Zoltron.

13. Flame throwers. 14. Hydraulic smash hammers. 15. The swamp witch will cast an Evil Spell on you. 16. Wormhole to a creepy planet. 17. Psychiatrist who will talk you into a DEEP depression. 18. Giga Worm. 19. Meeting of the Cannibal Psychopath Society with a sign on the door: 'We welcome uninvited guests'. 20. Five doors, all open, to confuse and scare you. 21. My private study room where I can finally work in peace.

1	1	2	3	2	4	3	5	6	4	7	8	5	9	6	10

11	7	12	8			9			10		11				12

EXPLANATION: START WITH TWO 1'S NEXT TO EACH OTHER. THEN WRITE TWO 2'S: LEAVING ONE OPENING BETWEEN. Fill it with a 3. As seen above, between 3 and 3 leave 2 open spaces. Fill it with a 4 (the 2 was already there). Between 4 and 4: create 3 open spaces. The 3 was already there, now write 5 and 6, and of course at the same time the second 5 and 6 on the right spot.

Continue until eternity... But of course, if you reach infinity, you'll have to write another infinity, infinitely far away, and then fill it with an infinite amount of numbers...

16 **CROSS SPACE**

PUZZLE: WHICH IS THE GREATEST "BLACK SPACE" created by surrounding crosses, in which you can't place a new cross? Here we reached 5.

ADDWAR

		1•		2•	
	1	6•	4		
5•	4•	6	3•	7	
	2	9	7•	3	
		9•	8•	8	
	5				

7	5•	1	9•	2•	2•
7	7	6•	6•	4	4•
5•	4•	6	3•	7	9
5	2	9	7•	3	3•
6	7	9•	8	8•	6
6	5	8	5•	7	2•

7	5•	1	9•	2•	2•
7	1	6•	6•	4	4•
5•	4•	6	3•	7	9
5	2	9	7•	3	3•
6	7	9•	8	8•	6
6	5	8	5•	7	2•

WE PLAY ON 6 BY 6 IN TWO COLORS (HERE ONE PLAYER GETS A DOT). Red and blue each place the digits 1 to 9 by turns. Then the adding starts. You may add up two digits of your own color, or one of your own and one of the enemy. Adding up may be done in a straight or diagonal line. However, you can't go over ten. So for example 7 + 9 = 6. Or 6 + 4 = 0. When you have to pass, the other player plays on. The winner is the one with the highest total.

EXAMPLES. 1. Start position. 2. First player: 6 + 1 is 7. Second player: 3 + 6 is 9. And this is how the game ends. The dot player had to pass once. 3. Simple method of counting: cross away equal numbers. Add up the rest. The non-dot player wins.

DECISION GRAPH

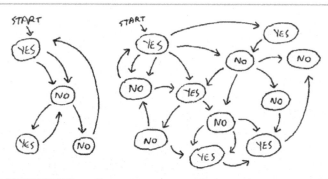

FOLLOW ANY ROUTE until you encountered 3 times a yes or a no. You can follow a path only once. Sometimes yes wins, sometimes no… However many different paths are possible.

19 CORNER HOOKS

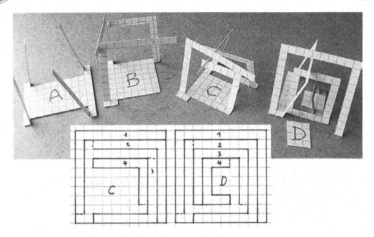

PAPER PUZZLE. Take a piece of light cardboard squared paper. If you don't find that, scan squared paper, enlarge it, and print it onto heavier paper. Or glue the paper onto cardboard. A. To fold up 4 corners we need a few cuts. B. Now we want to fold up a "hook" on each side. Puzzle: how to make the 4th corner ? Solution: C.

See also the drawing. D. Now with a second hook. Here again the puzzle was: how to make the 4th corner?

A lot more is to explore here!

20 PAPER TEAR NUMBERS

TRY TO INVENT SYSTEMS to write down numbers by tearing them into a piece of paper. In case someone important gives you her/his telephone number and you forgot your pen!

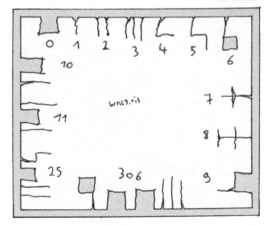

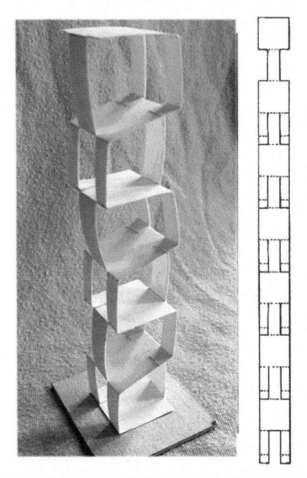

STILL MANY MORE VARIATIONS ARE POSSIBLE HERE.
(Solid lines need to be cut, dashed lines need to be creased and folded.)

THE STRAIGHT LINES ART STYLE

TRY TO DRAW FIGURES,
birds, dogs, landscapes…
with only straight lines. It is
a good exercise in learn-
ing to draw, and in seeing
things differently.

SQUARED PAPER NUMBERS

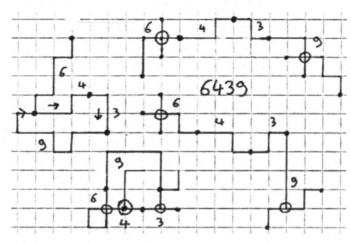

SMALL PASTIME SOLO GAME. Here we see 6439 on squared paper (change
the number as you wish). Each digit is translated into the same number of lines.
Try to make the diagrams as complex as possible.

TOZERO

-1	1		
		-1	
	1		

-1	1		
		-1	
	1		
2			

1+1=2

-1	1	1	-1	0
-1	1	-1	-1	-2
-1	1	-3	3	0
2	-3	3	-2	0
-1	0	0	-1	

SOLO GAME/PUZZLE. Play on a 4 x 4 grid. Now draw somewhere two "-1" and two "1." Then add two numbers up, and place the sum wherever you want. But you must avoid zero. When the whole board is full, add all your rows and columns. Then make the total sum. Here the result is - 4. The goal is to get as close to zero as possible.

25 **ARTIST BOOK**

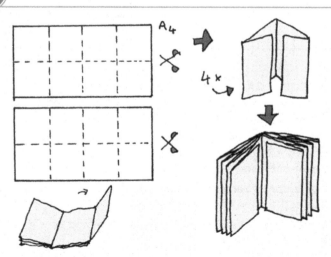

MAKE A SMALL BOOKLET or magazine. For 16 pages, use 2 A4 sheets. Fold and cut through the middle. Outer pages on the inside. You can print on one side. When on two sides, you can fold out 3 pages, and in the middle another 4 to make 32 pages.

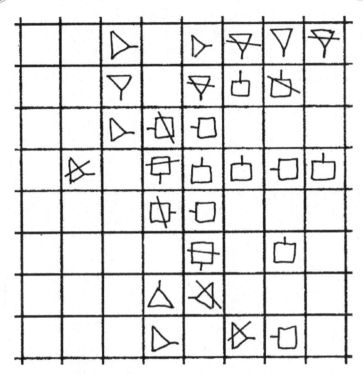

A SIMPLE SHOOTING GAME, which still needs some strategy. We play on 8 x 8. In turn blue and red (here triangle and square) put a tank somewhere. Players can shoot the enemy if their barrel points in the right direction.

In play, take turns to either shoot OR move your tank horizontally or vertically, until you meet an obstacle. At the same time you may change the direction of the barrel. Winner is the one with the most tanks left (real or virtual).

EXAMPLE: Square used a bad and too aggressive strategy, since you cannot shoot and move at the same time. Now he is excluded from the left side.

Result: the Triangle tanks can fill up the whole left side, and since it has occupied more squares, Triangle wins.

27 THE 20 LINES ART STYLE

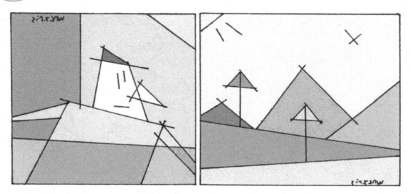

TRY TO DRAW LANDSCAPES AND PORTRAITS using only 20 straight lines.
Not only fun and a puzzle, but you may start to see the world differently!

28 ROLL STAPLE GAME

CUT A CARDBOARD KITCHEN PAPER ROLL in several "difficult" pieces.
Then try to assemble them in the right order (surprisingly difficult). Staple them
without glue.

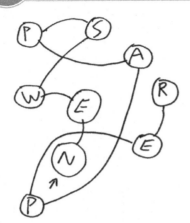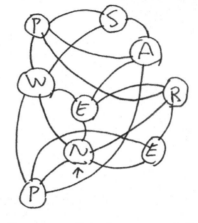

BOTH OPPONENTS CHOOSE (SECRETLY) A WORD with 9 letters. For example: "newspaper" or "computers." Then they write the letters on a piece of paper. See example. Now connect the letters in the right order to form the word "newspaper.' So 8 lines.

Then, to confuse the opponent, they may add 10 extra connections. The beginning letter is given. And then they each give their drawing to the opponent. Whoever guesses the right word first, wins. It is forbidden to use difficult or rare words. They must be likely to be known by your opponent.

30 **SCATTER GO**

JUST SCATTER SOME GO STONES on the Go board (a fantastic oriental game, the best board game ever invented), and start the game from there. You can do the same with chess or checkers/draughts.

A | 5 |
| 3 | 4 |
| 3 | 2 |
| 1 |
3/5

B | 6 | 7 |
	5	8	9
3	4
2	1
9

6	5
3	4	5
3	2
4	1
4/5/6

| 4 | 5 |
| 3 | 6 | 7 |
| 2 |
| 1 |
7

5	6	7
3	4
2	1
7

8	7
5	6
3	4
2	1
8

C

10	9	8	9	10	11	12	21	22
	7	8	✕	13	20	23
8	7	6	7		14	19
	5	8		15	18
2	3	4	9		16	17
1
8/9/10/23

18	17	16	15	14	13	12	13	16
		17	16	✕		11	14	15
20	19	18	7	8	9	10	11
			6		15	12
2	3	4	5		14	13
1
15/16/18/20

30	29	28	25	24	23	22	21	20
		27	26	✕		18	19
		8	9	10	11	12	17
		7	6		13	16
2	3	4	5		14	15
1
30

MATHEMATICAL PUZZLE. Draw a random dead end maze on squared paper, with 1 entrance. Start counting from 1, until you are blocked, either by a border, or by a previous number.

EXAMPLE A. You have 2 possibilities here: either go left after 2, and reach 3. Or go on to 5. 3 and 5 are the "potentials" of this cul-de-sac.

EXAMPLE B. Many more "potentials" and different paths, in this "squared paper cave."

EXAMPLE C. A more complex number cave with a hole in it. Even more potentials than mentioned are possible: 24, 27... But how to calculate in advance the potentials of such a cave, and the maximum number?

32 BAR FINDER

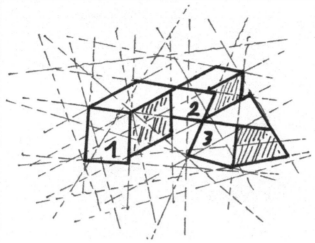

DRAW 25 RANDOM LINES (use a ruler) and then try to find a cube or a geometric bar (more or less) in it.

33 MIRROR REFLECTIONS

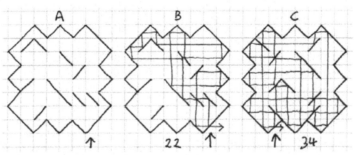

PASTIME DOODLE PUZZLE GAME, played on squared paper. Draw a board like example A above (around a 6 by 6 grid), drawing randomly 10 "mirrors", placed diagonally. And then we indicate a starting point.
Now imagine that a laser beam is projected from that point. It bounces to the mirrors or the sides,
and is reflected in a 90° angle. The goal is to return to the starting square, in as few turns as possible.

EXAMPLE A. How to draw the board around a 6 X 6 grid. And also the starting position.

EXAMPLE B. We count 22 reflections.

EXAMPLE C. 34 reflections.

34 ROPE CAR

YOU CAN MAKE SEVERAL OBJECTS and figurines with this kind of rather stiff, fluffy string. It is easy to drop some glue in joints if necessary.

35 CARDBOARD BOX FUN

DEXTERITY IS A BRAIN GAME TOO...

36 ANGLE POINTS

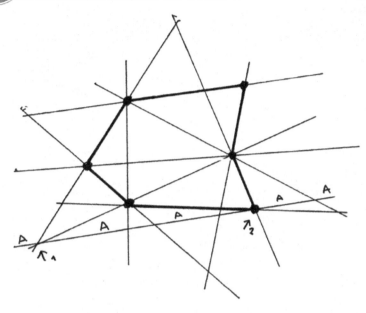

RANDOMLY DRAW 6 POINTS, then connect them using a ruler. The goal is to draw lines that intersect and create new points. However, points INSIDE the surface created by the 6 points don't count. You are allowed to connect with points OUTSIDE the surface, on the condition that at least ONE point is part of the original six. The goal is to create as many points as possible.

See line A: connects points 1 and 2. And 2 belong to the original six. Four new intersections are made here. Can it go on forever? In any case, this example is just the initial start…

SCRIBBLE DRAWINGS

DRAWING GAME.

All figures and landscapes can be transformed into scribbles.

Draw the scribbles and then let them come alive!

Row 1 (Example 1):

1	2	3
4	5	6
7	8	9

	2	3
5	5	6
7	8	9

	2	3
5	5	15
7	8	

	2	3
	10	15
7	8	

5		
	10	15
7	8	

	15	15
	15	

Row 2 (Example 2):

1	2	3
4	5	6
7	8	9

1	2	3
4	11	
7	8	9

1	2	3
15		
7	8	9

1	2	3
15		
15		9

Row 3 (Example 3):

2	7	9
3	6	5
8	4	1

2	7	
3	6	14
8	4	1

2	7	
3	6	15
8	4	

	9	
3	6	15
8	4	

3	15	15
8	4	

3	15	15
12		

SOLO PASTIME GAME.

We start with the 9 digits in a 3 by 3 square. If we add them all up we get 45, which can be divided in 3 times 15. Now we add up 2 neighboring digits, vertical or horizontal. We may write the sum in either of the two vacant places.

The goal is to end up with 3 lots of 15, as in Example 1.

Example 2: here we are blocked.

Example 3: here we changed the starting position of the digits.

Again we reach triple 15. Can we finish with 3 times a 15, on the same row or column? Yes!

39 AEIOU

VOWEL LANGUAGE GAME. Each opponent is given a vowel, for instance A. Now you must try to construct a sentence where every word starts with an A, or is preceded with only consonants.

"Wally was at that war, what a shame, and a wasted talent."

"Ho ho, no more of those cocktails brother, or you go home rolling over yourself."

Variation: make sentences with 15 to 20 words and use as many A's or O's as possible. Whoever has the most, wins.

40 PAPER MODEL OBJECTS

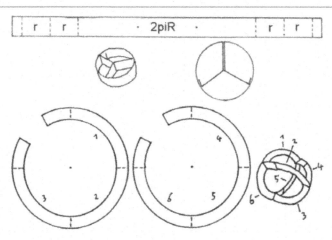

ON TOP: A SIMPLE WHEEL in 1 piece. Below: a ball object.

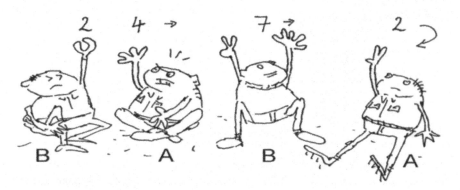

A GAME FOR 2 OR MORE PLAYERS. The first player holds up one finger. He plays "one." The second pops up 2 fingers. Then the game begins. From then on players add up the 2 previous digits. They have 2 choices: they can keep this digit, or add 1. They then show the chosen number with their fingers. If the digits go over ten, only the unit is used.

So for instance: 6 + 7 = 13, and this becomes 3. The first one who can reach zero, or 10, which equals zero, wins.

EXAMPLE (not the drawing):
A plays 1, B 2. A 3 (1 + 2), B 5 (2 + 3). Now B chose to keep 5. Six (he can add 1) would be a bad choice, since A gets then 3 + 6 = 9. And since he can add 1, he reaches zero.

EXAMPLE (drawing):
A now adds 1 to his 3 = 4. B has 6 (4 + 2) and adds 1 = 7. A has 7 + 4 = 1 and he adds 1 = 2. B gets 2 + 7 = 9 and he adds 1 = 0.

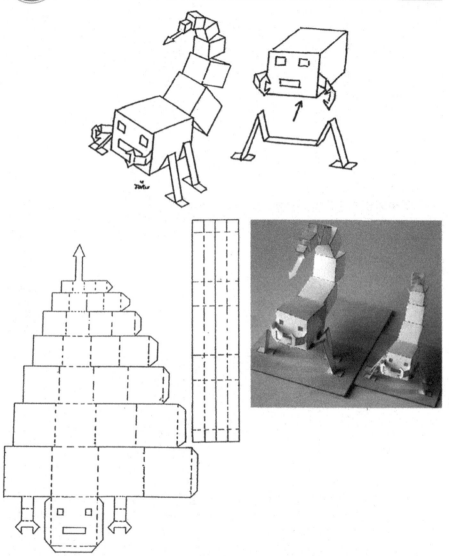

PAPER TEMPLATE. Solid lines need to be cut, dashed lines need to be creased. The paws are folded double and the feet set apart for more strength and stability.

HOOK DOODLE

LITTLE PASTIME SOLO GAME. Try to fill a given board on squared paper with as many "Hook Doodles" as possible. But remember, if there is a "hidden" Hook Doodle on the borders (any part of which is showing), that also counts for one.

 ## ALIEN WORMS

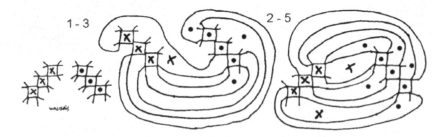

THIS IS A VERY SIMPLE GAME, but it's fun. Draw 2 "alien worms", like the left hand drawing. The x and the dot set of worms each has 16 "paws." Now link paw to paw, Cross worm to Dot worm.

Players may not connect with their own paws. Lines may not cross. Freestanding paws that point into a closed area may claim that area. This is 1 point. As long as connections are still possible you are obliged to play on.

45 SIXFOLD

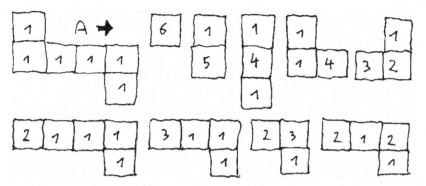

SOLITAIRE PASTIME DRAWING GAME. Draw all the POSSIBLE folds you can make from the original blueprint of a cube. See example: still many more to go...

46 NON-MAGICAL SQUARE

1	6	5	12
4	2	7	13
3	8	9	20
8	16	21	12

10

7	6	5	18
4	1	8	13
3	2	9	14
14	9	22	17

9 / 10

13	2	8	3
20	4	7	9
12	6	5	1
16	12	20	13

EVERYBODY KNOWS A MAGIC SQUARE, where the sum of all sides plus the diagonals are equal to each other. But...if we write the numbers 1 to 9 totally randomly in these 9 squares, and we add them up...we always seem to have at least two equal numbers. Now, can I construct a totally "non-magical" square like this, but where all the sums are different?

35

47 ## SCRIBBLE PANORAMAS

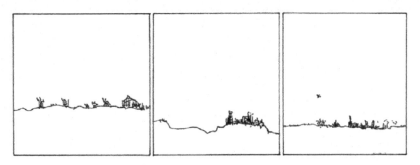

ART GAME. Draw distant horizons with nearly unrecognizable details in it. Something that looks like a house, or a forest, or...

 48 ## MIRROR DRAWING GAME

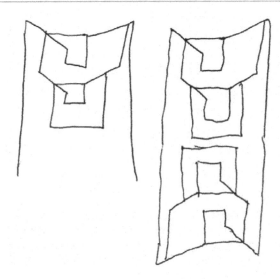

CHALLENGE: draw a mirror image of a complicated abstract drawing.

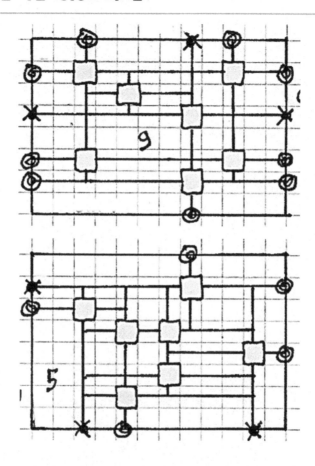

SOLO GAME. We draw a field of 12 by 8 on squared paper. Next we draw 7 squares randomly on the board. Then we connect these squares with the lines at the border. Each square MUST have four departing lines. Then we count.

In Example 1 there are 12 connections with the borderlines. But each line that is touched by 2 other lines becomes invalid (a "cross" also counts for two lines). So only 9 valid connections remain. The goal is of course to create as many as possible.

Example 2: only 5 connections.

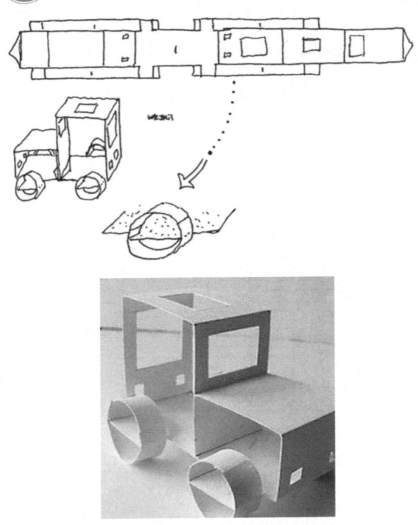

ALSO A PUZZLE! First, figure out which lines need to be cut or creased and folded. Note: the template includes flaps for gluing. Each piece for the wheels needs to be curved with a dull knife. When drawn freehand, the car has a more artsy effect.

51 LITTLE PAPERMEN

DO NOT CUT OUT EYES AND MOUTH if you want to paint it, but glue them on. The separated feet give stability. Draw it freehand on light cardboard for a more lively appearance. Solid lines need to be cut, dotted lines to be creased (using a dull knife). You need small scissors and a sharp knife, with tweezers to press the glued parts. (A: upper leg is left open).

52 CONTINUOUS LINE DRAWINGS

ART GAME. Try to use only straight lines.

53 PENTA-TRIANGLE

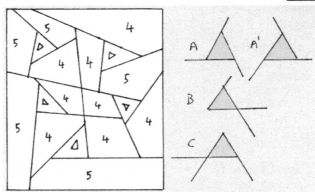

SOLO GAME. First, draw a rectangle, and then put 5 triangles randomly into it. Next, extend the sidelines of the triangles. However, these extended lines are stopped by any previously drawn lines. We must use a ruler for all this. The extension of the sidelines must be done in the right direction.

Example A and his mirror-image A' are correct. B and C are wrong. Goal is to make as many spaces as possible. There is 1 point for each of the sides of the shapes formed. Here we reach a total of 57.

54 PAPER ROCKET

CUT THE SOLID LINES and score and fold the dotted lines

55 NUMBER BLOCK SPIRAL

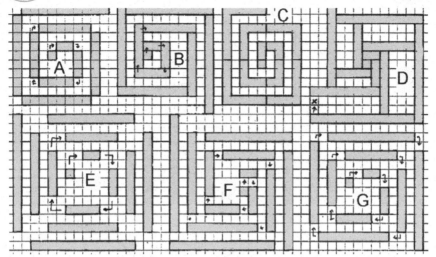

GEOMETRIC SOLO GAME AND PUZZLE. Try different systems to rotate "number blocks" - blocks of an increasing number of squares. Sometimes you are blocked, like in example D.

But there are many more possibilities to explore. For example, with the expansion of the number blocks you can also let the distances between them grow.

56 WIRE WAYS

IMAGINE THAT THE CUBES on the left are open and made out of iron wire. In the second drawing, we see that there are 3 connected cubes on top, one in the middle, and only 2 beneath.

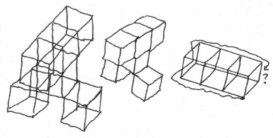

Challenge: now imagine that you must make this out of one long iron wire. How would you do that, and which is the most efficient way, without too many double connections?

41

↓2   5↙

				13
			14	12
3	2	1		11
4	15			10
5	6	7	8	9

3→   ←1   4↑

↘3   ↓8   5↙

6	5	4	3	14
22	7	2	15	13
23	1	8		12
24	16	21	9	11
17	18	19	20	10

→6   ←2   ↗1   4↑   7↖

SOLO GAME PUZZLE. We play on a 5 x 5 grid. First, write down a number 1 somewhere. Then choose one out of eight possible directions (you may use a direction only once). See examples.

Then count from 1 in that specific direction. If you encounter a previous number, you can jump over it, and then count further. The goal is to create the highest possible number.

In example A we are blocked at 15. None of the three remaining directions can be used. But in B we reach 19.

42

NUMBERJUMP

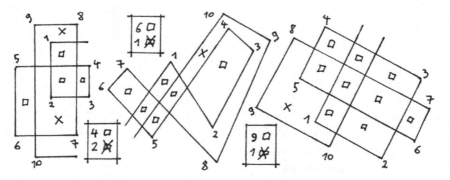

SOLO PUZZLE GAME, on a grid of 5 x 5. Randomly we place 4 zeros on the board, and one number 1. With each turn the digits may move one square further, straight or diagonal. However, they stay the same number. It is only when they can jump over a zero that they increase by one digit. The goal is to reach 10.

EXAMPLES. Starting position: 1 jumps over zero and becomes 2. That 2 needs first to move diagonally right under to jump over a zero and become 3. Here we can even reach 10 twice. Last grid: impossible to reach 10.

59 RECTANGLE GENERATOR

PASTIME DOODLE GAME. You may change the direction of the line 10 times, in a more or less straight line. Every rectangle you create is 1 point, a space that is not a rectangle is minus 1 point.

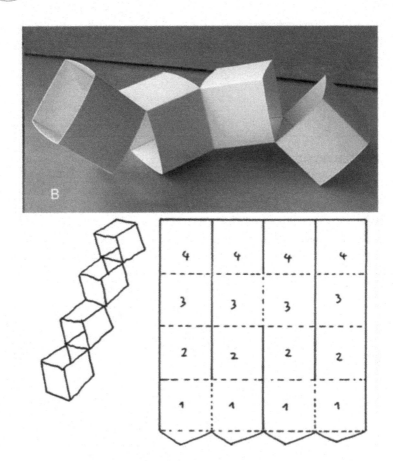

ALL NUMBERS ARE ON THE OUTSIDE. Perfect for an artist booklet or display, since no recto verso copy is needed. Solid lines need to be cut, dashed lines need to be creased. And, it can be folded flat.

PAPERMAN TWO

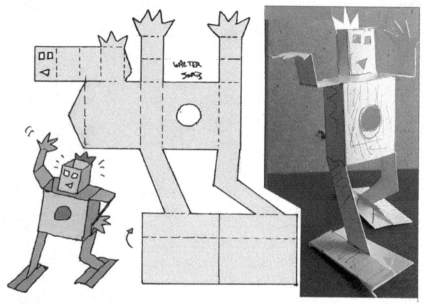

DRAW THE PATTERN FREEHAND, this gives a much more lively effect. This is also a "FlatFold" model – it can be folded flat and sent by mail. The Paperman to the right is an example model – yours will look different.

62

HOOK CREATURES

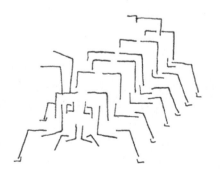

DRAWING PASTIME GAME.
Trying to draw something within certain restrictions and rules is always a challenge. For example. drawing on a very small piece of paper, like a stamp. Or using dust mixed with water and even glue. In this example, we try to create something like a "Hook Scorpion" using only "hooks".

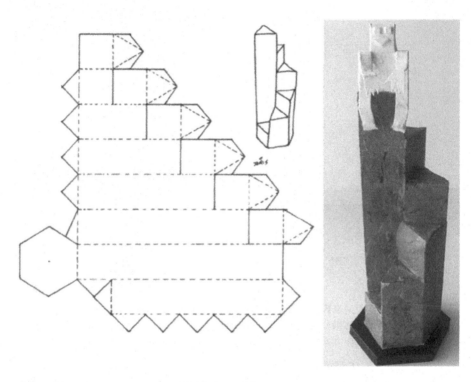

CUT SOLID LINES, score and fold dotted lines.

EXTREMELY FAST LITTLE GAME. One player puts number 10 below right on a 6 x 6 grid. See drawing.

From there on he may move one square, horizontally or diagonally. Each time his digit goes down. But there is also his opponent: the X. When 10 reaches the left side of the field and can place a zero there, he has won. However, X tries to prevent that: whenever X draws his mark next to a digit, that digit must jump over the X, and of course, loses 1 in value. X however may ONLY put his mark when there is the possibility for such a jump. Otherwise, he must hold off. Moreover, X is NOT obliged to play.

SEE EXAMPLE. 10 was able to play down to 3. Now he has three possibilities to put a 2. Unfortunately, each time X can prevent him from reaching zero on the left side. So X won.

RECTANGLE ENTANGLE

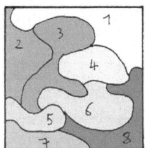
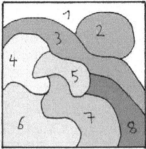

EACH PLAYER HAS A PAPER RECTANGLE of the same dimensions. Then, with scissors, they cut them in 8 "difficult" pieces. They mix the pieces up, turn them over, and so on. Then the other player may solve this puzzle. The first one to complete the rectangle, wins.

This can be made more easy by only allowing straight lines to cut the pieces. Or more difficult by cutting 10 pieces.

66 **FLAT FOLD DRAGONFLY**

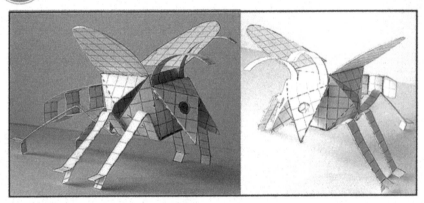

THIS MODEL CAN BE FOLDED FLAT and sent in an envelope by mail. It should be made out of colored light cardboard pieces.

Challenge: can you by "reverse engineering" draw the templates? Wings, head, collapsible cube, 3 sets of (double folded) legs, 3 pieces for the tail, antenna? Draw it freehand, this gives a more lively effect.

DISPLAY TEMPLATE

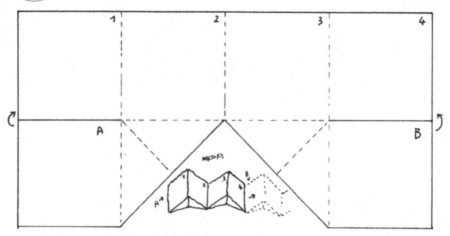

THIS DESIGN CAN BE USED TO MAKE A MAGAZINE, an artist's book, a display… Each time you get 4 pages to the front. Several variations are possible. You can extend the flaps at the front to a square, as the rest. Although that page is then folded diagonally when the "book" opens. A and B are glued to the back of 1 and 4, but can also be used to extend the booklet.

68

STRIPE TYPES

DOODLE PASTIME GAME. The drawing says it all. Mirror images and tilted images are all valid here. I do wonder however how to calculate all variations.

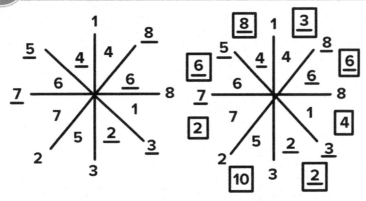

FIRST, DRAW THE CROSS AND X TO MAKE THE STAR SHAPE. Then in turn blue and red write a digit down, from 1 to 8 (here in black/white: underlined and not). They can write a number at the end of a line, or in a segment. When the "compass card" is full, then the counting begins. For each of the eight segments separately the three numbers are counted and subtracted from each other. Whoever reaches the biggest total number, wins.

EXAMPLES: 1. The finished game. 2. The counting. Underlined wins.

70 **DECAGON DOODLE**

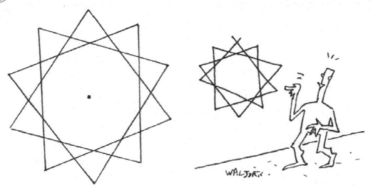

WALJDRK.

DOODLE GAME. Try to draw a decagon, a polyhedron with 10 sides, in this form, freehand, and very fast. It is a challenge! But when you master it, you can draw it for your friends, seemingly randomly.

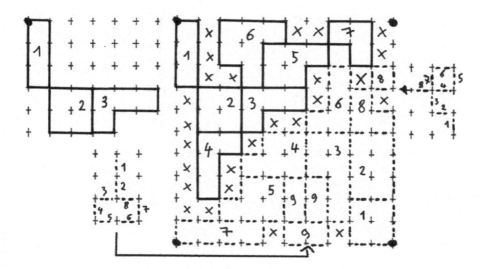

WE PLAY IN 2 COLORS, ON A 10 BY 10 FIELD (here solid and dotted line). One player starts upper left, the other bottom right. Each time you have to build a "castle" with exactly 8 lines, and that surface needs to be enclosed.

Also, you need to start from one of your own previous angle points. See for instance solid line 3: it is 8 lines plus 2 already existing at the right of castle 2. You may touch the angle points of your opponent. See second field: solid line reaches castle 7, but now he is blocked.

Dotted line may play on. He can draw castles 8 and 9. They're a bit unusual, but they are in accordance with the rules of the game. The crossed-out squares are invalid. Dotted line has the most squares in his castles, and wins.

72 SQUARE ROLL

(grid 1 side numbers) 1 1 2 / 6 1 4

(grid 2 side numbers) 3 3 2 / 4 2 5

(grid 3 side numbers) 1 1 4 / 5 4 3 / 3 2 1 / 6 5 4

MORE OF A GAME OF CHANCE, although some strategy is needed. Draw a 6 x 6 grid. Roll 3 dice at the same time. With each throw, you fill the empty squares with your results. BUT: that must be done in 3 DIFFERENT rows. However, when you do a second roll you may use previously occupied rows, on the condition that you again use 3 different rows.

You may throw the dice as many times as you want. The goal is to complete the whole square. The difference, negative or positive, plus the unused numbers, are penalty points.

EXAMPLE. 1. Player did 2 rolls. The thick lines show the dividing lines. 2. After 4 rolls, two squares stay open. The score is minus 2 (no unused numbers). 3. A bad ending. With his last roll player can put his 5 in the bottom row. But he can't put his 6 and 4 anywhere.
Result: (- 2 - 2 - 3) + (- 6 - 4) = - 17.

73 MIRROR SENTENCE

LANGUAGE GAME.

Write a sentence and then stop, and go on to complete the sentence with a version of the same words as in the first part. "The fox chased the rabbits, but then he stumbled over the cat, but then the cat, he chased the rabbits, over the stumbled fox."

74 ROPE FACES

CREATE FACES WITH ROPES HANGING FROM TREES. It's "Land Art." Take pictures. And then leave them like that. Imagine the amazement of future hikers walking the forest.

75 SUBLEVEL 5

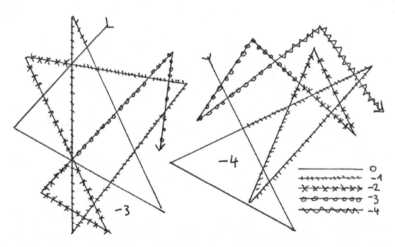

WE DRAW 10 CONTINUOUS LINES, more or less randomly, crossing each other. We start from ground level Zero. When we need to cross that level, we go one down: minus 1. And so on. Can we reach sublevel 5? (This game really should be done in several colors.)

TWO CUBES PROBLEM

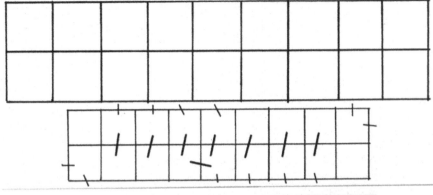

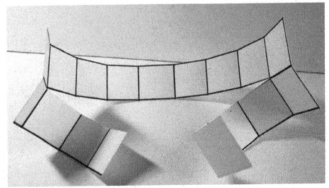

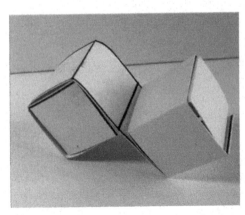

HOW TO CUT AND FOLD THIS TEMPLATE SO THAT YOU GET 2 CUBES ATTACHED TO EACH OTHER? See the solution underneath. The fold lines with a thick stripe need to be cut, the other creased and folded.
Some faces of the cubes will be doubled. If you want a better finish, add flaps.
These triangular flaps should be drawn where indicated by the thin stripes on the outline.

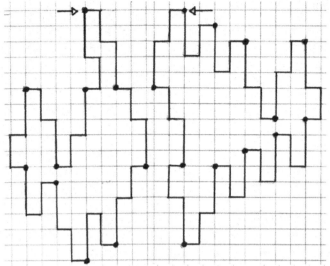

SOLO PASTIME. Play on squared paper. Try to find paper with bigger squares, or scan it, enlarge it, print several. They're useful for a lot of things. We start with the arrow. Each time you move 1 square, horizontally, then 2 squares vertically, one horizontal, and 3 vertical again. And this in any chosen direction. The goal is to "close" the tower.

78 **RETURNING DOMINOES**

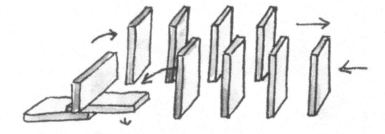

PUZZLE: HOW TO CHANGE THE DIRECTION OF FALLING DOMINOES
with 3 extra dominoes? See example. Taking half a turn works with the same system, by setting the first row at a diagonal.

79 WOBBLE WHEEL

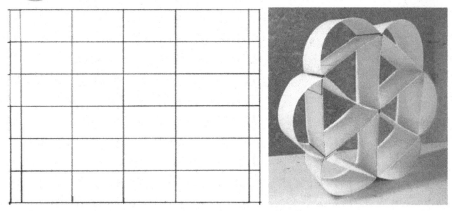

DESIGNING ALL KINDS OF NEW WHEELS IS FUN...
See template: hexagon with a bump on top. The hexagon alone, consisting of 6 triangles glued together as a wheel, is interesting.

80 VIRUS

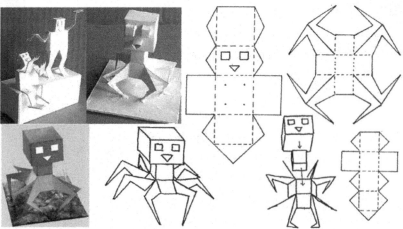

SAYS ONE PAPERMAN TO THE OTHER: "my virus was THAT big." Ideally the legs should be done in a bit stronger cardboard. This model can also be a spider, hanging from a thread.

56

FIRST, MIX ALL THE DOMINOES. Then, randomly, stack them in groups of 4. There will be 7 of them. Now you may lay a domino on top of another if 1 of the numbers is equal. For example: if a 3-1 is on top of a stack, you may lay that domino on top of another stack with a 6-1. You are allowed to create new stacks, even when it's only 1 domino. You may also cut a stack in two.

The goal is to form 1 stack containing all the dominoes. It is of course possible that underneath an existing stack, not all the dominoes have a corresponding number.

SEE EXAMPLE. 1. Starting position, with already one domino ready to lay on top of another stack (0-6 on 6-6). 2. Game and stacks in evolution. 3. Stack towards the player is growing. 4. The big stack below is cut in two, for practical reasons. 5. Big stack cut in three. 6. Result: one big stack in three parts.

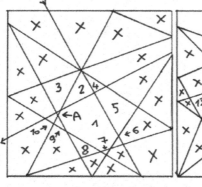
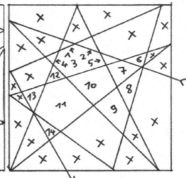

DRAW A SQUARE USING A RULER. Then draw 10 continuous lines from one side to another. Imagine that you have to cut out all the interior polygons, but without compromising the exterior frame of the square. The parts that'll do that are marked with an X.

Try to make as many interior surfaces as possible. Example 1: 10 pieces. (See A: a surface that is too small doesn't count. That is seen as a "point". Try to avoid them while drawing).

Example 2: we reach 14.

83 INCREASE AND DECREASE

FIRST, WRITE A SENTENCE WHERE THINGS ARE TINY, and then rewrite the same sentence, but with everything blown out of proportion. Make it into a game.
"A mouse crawled out of the tiny hole in the wooden wall and tripped to the chunk of cheese and nibbled a small piece of it."
"Twenty elephants stormed out of the enormous crack in the reinforced concrete and thundered to the mountain of cheese and devoured everything greedily."
"A barely visible tiny fly looked through the microscopic hole in the mosquito

net and fluttered slowly to the molecule of cheese to suck it up a bit." And now make it bigger than the twenty elphants, make it ENORMOUS...

58

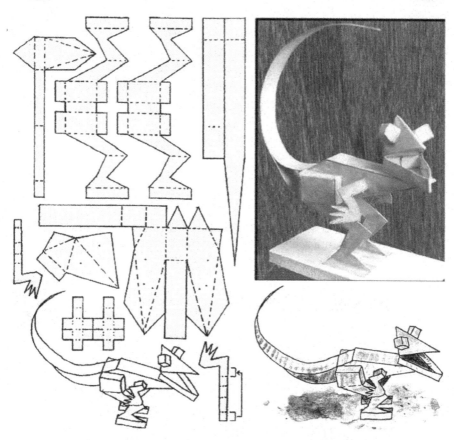

ATTENTION: THE TWO ARMS ARE FOLDED IN A MIRROR-IMAGE.

The thighs are open. The lower legs are double for strength, and the feet are separated, for stability. The tail is also partly open, and needs to be creased with a dull knife to make it curl.

This model can be painted.

Now, designing such templates is certainly a "Brain Game." And of course, you should invent, draw, and make your own models.

85　MENTAL KNOTS

ALWAYS START THE DAY WITH A PUZZLE. Is this knot a real or a false one? First try to solve it mentally and visually. Then pull both ends.

86　ISLAND OR BRIDGE

O	O	▓	X	X	O	O	O	X	O
X	O	X	O	X	X	O	O	X	▓
X	X	X	O	X	X	X	X	O	X
O	O	O	O	O	X	O	O	O	O
O	X	X	O	X	X	X	X	X	O

IN TURNS, X AND O PUT THEIR MARKS ON A FIELD OF 5 BY 5.
One square is left open, so each player has 12 turns. The winner is the one with a connection from side to side, horizontal or vertical. OR, when that is not possible, the largest contiguous area of squares that border each other straight (so not diagonally).
Examples: A. It's clear that on the fourth row, O has such a connection. She wins. B. No connection here. But X has an area of 9 squares. And O only 6. He wins.

87 POCKET FOLDING

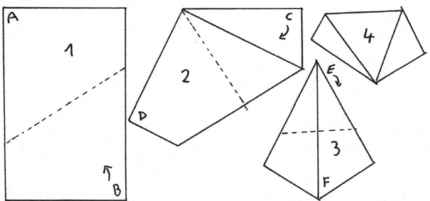

ORIGAMI PUZZLE. Go to the library, borrow a book by Tolstoy, and tear out 1 page (too many pages anyway). (This is a joke !!). I mean: take a blank page and bring point B to A. Then C to D. Now you have 2 "pockets." Defined as a "sac" where you can put something in, like a small ball, and that ball won't fall out. You may hold the paper in different directions.

Now fold E to F. Result in picture 4. This has 5 "pockets" (1 pocket divided into 2). Can you reach 10 with a minimum of folds?

88 TWO EYES DOODLES

PASTIME DOODLE GAME. Try to find as many variations as possible on this "hooks" design.

TRY TO CREATE VERY THIN FIGURES (or a helicopter) out of light cardboard. It's a bit like drawing lines in space. Fun.

DRAW A 6 X 6 GRID. In black/white we use arrow A and arrow B with a line at the bottom. A starts top left, B bottom right. They both draw an arrow in the direction they want. For their next moves, they must: 1. follow the direction of their previous arrow and 2. that new arrow must point in THE SAME DIRECTION as the previous move of the opponent.

See example. A 3 goes one square down as is indicated by arrow one. However, that arrow must be UPWARDS, since B 2 is also upwards. Now A 3 is blocked. When that happens he gets a free choice. He may move to a new adjacent square (not diagonal). And his new arrow may be in ANY direction. See A 5. But that then means that B 6 has to place his arrow also downwards…

Then he gets a free choice: B 8. The goal is to reach the highest number.

Example 1. The game is over since it is clear that A will reach a higher number than B (more space). Example 2. B will win.

91 FLOCK OF BIRDS

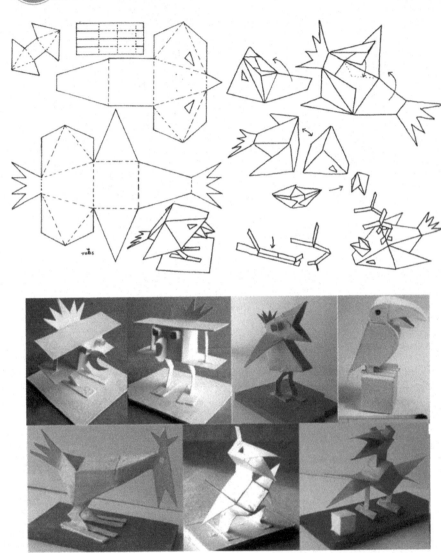

TEMPLATE FOR A SMALL BIRD. Designing all kinds of other birds will certainly become a Brain Game. And do the Biplane Birds really exist? Some say they do…

92 · MOUSE IN THE HOUSE

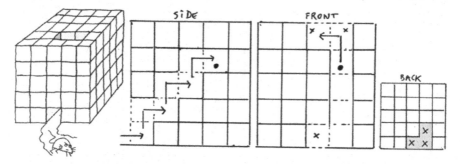

PUZZLE. OUR HOUSE IS A BLOCK OF 5 X 5 X 5 CUBES. The mouse enters at the back and wants to pass through all 4 floors before she leaves through the entrance. However, the mouse can only jump one cube high.

How many cubes do we need to remove? We see on the drawings that at the back 3 cubes are gone, one at the front, and two in the ceiling. Now look at the drawing "Side." It's clear that, to climb the stairs, also the ceiling needs to be higher, otherwise our mouse is blocked. And then the little creature reaches the 3rd floor.

But to reach the 4rd, two cubes need to be removed. But since there are no gaps at the side of the building, the mouse must have changed direction. See drawing "Front." After that, the animal retraces her steps all the way. But to reach the front of the building an extra corridor is needed.

Conclusion: to reach the 3rd floor, 7 blocks needed to be removed. To the 4rd floor: 2. And the hallway through the middle of the building: 5.

ZAPLINE

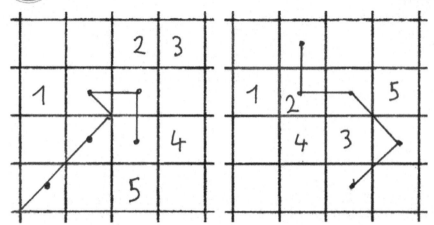

WE PLAY ON 4 X 4 IN TWO COLORS. Let's say that left here is red, and right blue. Red draws, not visible for blue, a continuous "Zapline" of 5 squares. And then he places 5 red numbers on the board, freely chosen. Blue does the same.

Then they compare the result. The blue Zapline, when drawn on the red board, destroys the red numbers 4 and 5. And the red Zapline will kill blue 4, 2, 3. Red wins. Of course, this is more a game of chance, but some psychological insight may help…

94 WING STAR

TRY TO DRAW THIS LINE STAR AS FAST AS POSSIBLE.
Do it freehand of course. You should have several complicated freehand patterns in your head and your hand. Amaze people with it.

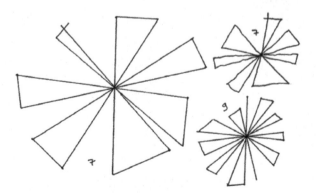

66

∏+∏→ ∏∏ ⊔∏ ┌⊬ ⊬┐ ⊓ ⅊

∏ ┌⊓ ⊕┐ ┌⊬ ⊬┐ ∏ ⊡ ┌∏⊋

⊕⌐ ⌐⊕ ⊕⌐ ∏⊏ ⊐∏ ∏ ∏ ⊔⊔
                      ⊔∏ ⊔∏

⊡ ⊌∃ ⊢⊣ ⊢⊣ ⊔⊢ ∏ ┌∏ ⊐⊏ ⊏⊏

∣∏⊔⌐ ⊔∃⊔┐ ┌⊔∏ ┌∏ ∏ ⊡

∏ ┌∏⊕┐ ┌⊋⊢⊣ ⊕∏ ⌐⊕⌐∣ ⊔⊕

⊔⊕⌐ ⊡ ⊌∃ ⊢⊣ ⊔⊢ ⊔⊢ ∏ ┌∏ ⊔⊬

⊔⌐ ┌⊬ ⊬∏ ┌∏ ┌∏⊕┐∣∏∣ ∏⊏

⊐∏ ⊏∏ ⊐⊏ ⊐⊐ ⊐⊏ ...

DRAWING GAME. Try to find as many variations as possible. This can also be done as a game among friends (or solo) against the clock, with the winner being the one with the most valid variations in a given time. (Valid… because it is very easy to draw the same variation twice.)

	X			
		X		

1	X	5	X	O
2	O	X	O	X
3	X	O	X	4
X	O	X	X	O
O	I	II	O	X

WITH EACH MOVE, A PLAYER PLACES TWO MARKS. And they must be connected diagonally in one of the surrounding squares. They play until it becomes impossible to make such a move. Then open territory is counted. When surrounded by more X than O, X may claim it. He gets a point for every square. See example. X reaches 5, and O has only 2. The board of 5 by 5, here shown, is a bit too small. The first player has a certain advantage.

So, for the second game, change that. All in all, a very simple and fast, but amusing game.

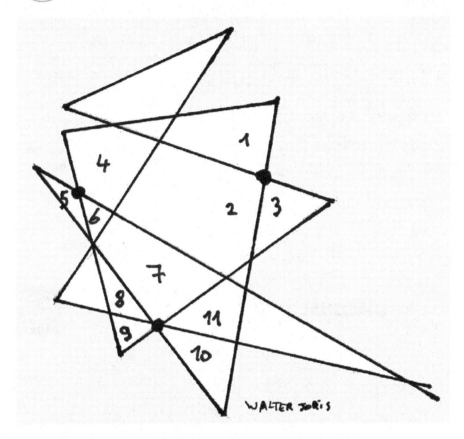

FIRST DRAW 10 STRAIGHT, CONTINUOUS LINES. And then CLOSE the figure with the 10th line. Next choose and highlight 3 angle-points on this figure. Any closed surface that contains one of these points at one of his angles gives you 1 point.

How many surfaces can you maximally score? And how many more points than the highlighted 3 do you need to cover ALL the possible surfaces made by 10 lines? (A surface may only be counted once.)

LANGUAGE GAME. AROUND THE TABLE, everybody stands up in turn and tells a hesitating, uncertain story.

1. There was no...murder...I think. But some say...you know... But it isn't. As far as I can remember at least. I thought so. But the police say otherwise. So maybe it was... This means that there eventually could be...a kind of murder. But it isn't certain. In fact, it's doubtful. What do you think? Anyway, I haven't seen a dead body yet. Unless I keep annoying you guys with my story much longer. But how long? I think it can last forever, if forever even exists.

2. It's true, when I was in the Alps, I saw these...you know. And then they came. It was too late anyway. But not too soon either. The cows then attacked the... Well, at least they didn't attack the crocodiles. But then how could there be crocodiles in the Alps? This makes the story a bit unbelievable. But somebody moved, that's certain. Was it?.. No, I don't think so. 'We must get our...' 'said the Austrian farmer. 'And then...' And he made it clear with his hands. But I didn't understand it.

The winner? I'm not sure...whoever you decide!

99   PAPER TEAR CARS

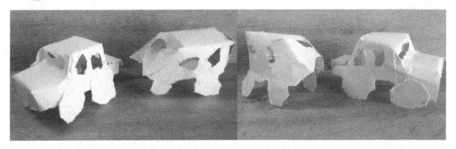

CUT PAPER WITH YOUR HANDS, without scissors, to form cars, figures, planes… Do all this with maybe just the aid of a friendly glue stick.

100   HEXAGON SHIFT

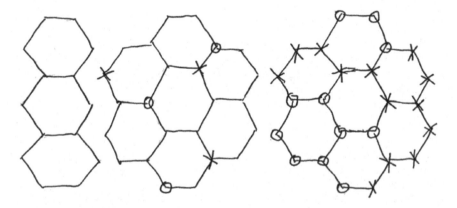

DRAW THE BOARD FREEHAND: first 3 hexagons on top of each other. Then add the four others. Circle and cross place each, in turn, 3 marks. Only one of them may be on the middle hexagon. From then on they may move to a neighboring point. When one is blocked, the other plays on.

The goal is to reach the most marks. See example: Cross has 13, Circle has 11.

DOMINO BLOCK

IS IT POSSIBLE TO LAY THE DOMINOES so that they form a block of 4 long and 7 high, so that each Domino rests on top of another that has at least 1 corresponding number?

And further, that the top set of Dominoes show numbers from 0-1/2-3/4-5/6-0? Yes, see (one of the) solutions. Can you find others?

102 LINE DIGIT

EACH PLAYER DRAWS A 4 X 4 GRID and places the digit 1 to 4 in it. This is given to the opponent. Now he/she has to choose a starting point, and from there on trace a continuous line. That line must border digit 1 only with one side…and so on. See example. Lines may not overlap.

The winner is the one who can do this and, even better, return to the starting point. If not, the winner is the one who has all the numbers right. This is the case in the first example. However, the opponent succeeded in the return to the point of origin.

103 INFINITE LOOP STORIES

TRY TO TELL, WITH FRIENDS, each a story that will always repeat itself.

The cat ran after the mouse, but the mouse ran towards the dog for protection, and then the dog chased the cat. But the cat ran towards the rabbit. And then the dog forgot about the cat and tried to catch the rabbit. So then the cat could go after the mouse again. But the mouse again ran towards the dog...

104 THE DUPE

"A SMALL CUBE IS ALWAYS THE DUPE," says the small cubes. And indeed: in this staple game every big cube needs to stand on 1 small cube. The goal is to achieve the highest tower. But...it'll have to be stable. Here we use seven cruel Big Cubes to crush 7 small ones. This should be made into a physical game with 20 big and 20 small cubes.

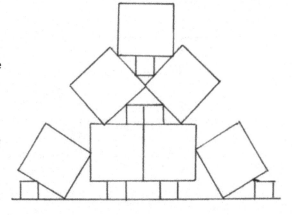

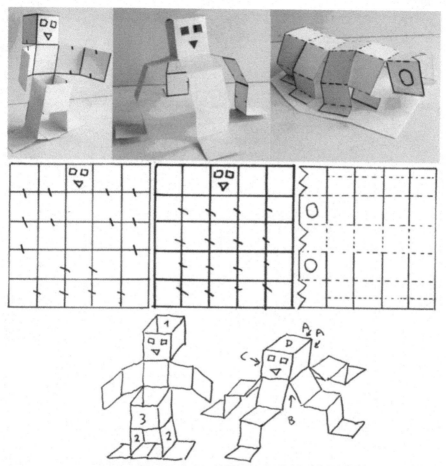

THESE ARE 'FOLD CREATURES' MADE OUT OF SQUARES. "Imagine millions of us", they say, "since we can be stored flat, and produced very fast. Provide us with 'flat neurons' and let us absorb solar energy and (human?) MEAT, and we will conquer the universe."

See first picture. 1 and 3 are glued together. The two squares between the legs are folded backwards and upwards and provide strength. The legs are doubled and the feet separated. All lines with a stripe (or solid lines for number 3) need to be cut, the others, creased and folded.

106 COIN BILLIARDS

TAKE TWO RETRACTABLE BALLPOINT CLICK PENS with a button on the side. Hold them against a coin, to shoot it away. You can use heads or tails of identical coins, but here we use 6 big coins against 10 smaller ones. Still some strategy needed.

107 SQUARES DRAWING

ART GAME. Try to draw figures, street scenes, or here: birds of prey, with only little squares.

FIRST DRAW TEMPLATE A, WITH HIS FLIP SIDE. Cut it out and crease all the folds. Draw it freehand, it's not meant to be perfect art. You are going to fold it like in the drawing underneath. The result will be a square.

But before you do that, imagine the portrait you want to draw. And what parts of that picture, on which squares, on which side? Here it is already given, but of course, there are more possibilities.

So this is a pastime brain puzzle. See template B. The folds with two stripes on them need to be cut. You will end up with a 2 by 3 rectangle. And on that, you want to draw this little man.

Furthermore, for both templates: how many different drawings can you make? Can you use all squares?

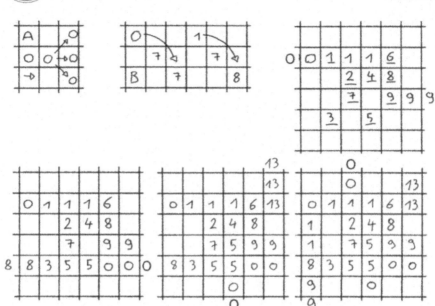

SOLO GAME. DRAW RANDOMLY THE DIGITS 1 TO 9 on a 6 x 6 grid. Then start with a zero in a chosen direction (from one side of the grid to the other), and try to reach the highest number. You must always follow that direction (straight or diagonally), or doing so, jump over any digit. Then you can add two digits up. See examples 1 and 2 for how this works.

After a specific direction is done, you must start with a zero in another direction. The sequence of the directions or the starting point is free. See example 3. The underlined digits are the ones that were already drawn. Zero jumps over 1, stays 1. Goes one case further, and then jumps over 8 and becomes 9. That 9 goes one further and moves outside the grid. After the four directions are done in this example, a total sum of 39 outside the grid is achieved.

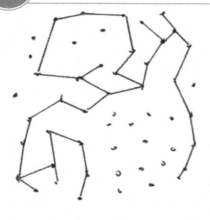
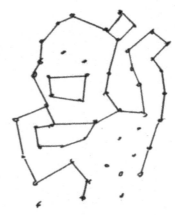

DRAWING PASTIME GAME. Draw 50 random points, and then try to discover a figure in it. Here we see: "Tweezer Hands Man" and "Thinker with Hat."

Also an exercise in fantasy.

111 **EIGHTCUT**

CUT AN A4 PAPER IN 8 PIECES using a scissors and straight cuts. Then try to compose a recognizable "something." The pieces may be turned, and laid over each other. You may draw one or two "eyes."

Collage game.

Walter Joris

IF YOU HAVE DIFFICULTY DRAWING ANIMALS AND HUMANS, just make them 3-dimensional.

It's easier to picture that in your mind.

(113) SPACE FOLDS

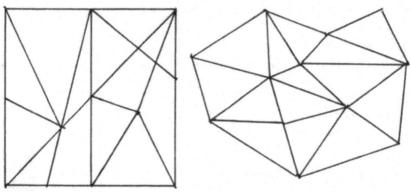

PASTIME PUZZLE. Draw several straight-line divisions in a square. Or draw randomly several triangles. See example: both 14 pieces.

Now try to cut (scissors) and fold (crease) them so that you get an "abstract sculpture," but still IN ONE PIECE.

114 BLUE CATCH

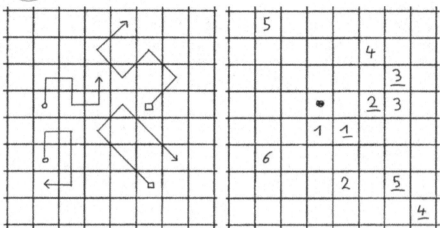

SHOULD BE PLAYED WITH 2 COLORS ON A 8 X 8 GRID. The game starts with blue putting a thick point somewhere. Blue can move 5 squares further, but only straight. See example.

There he puts a digit. Here, the underlined digits are those of red. Red can also go 5 further, but only diagonally. That is the starting point for blue AND red. Now red tries to capture blue (i.e. the last digit blue has written).

Squares that are occupied cannot be passed anymore. In the example, red 5 is blocked, and cannot make 5 diagonal moves anymore. Red loses.

115 SPEAR THROWER

LEARN TO PRACTICE the ladle-fork spear-thrower (Atlatl).

Away from other people, of course.

116 POINT CROSSING

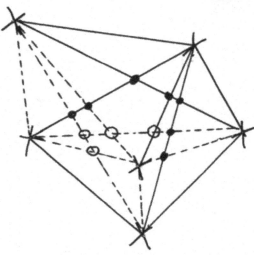

START WITH SIX CROSSES. These are the original starting points. This fast, unpretentious game needs to be played with two colors. Here we use solid and dashed lines. First each player connects 2 cross-points. The other player is next, and so on, until all points are connected (5 departing lines from each original point). Whenever a line crosses another, the player may claim that new point. Here we use a thick point and an open circle. It is forbidden to take a "detour." The connecting line must be "straight," more or less. In the example: Solid Line made 7 dots and Dashed Line only 4. The first player has a slight advantage, so you play two games.

117 DRESSING UP STICKMAN

CHILDREN WILL LOVE THIS LITTLE GAME. See Stickman and now dress him up. Rules: it must be done with more or less straight lines, and all must be "attached" to Stickman. Eyes, hair, ears, smile, hat, antenna, hands, spear, pants, cup of coffee, shoes, ground, shirt, suspenders, shirt pockets, Walkman, grass, loose shoelace, wristwatch, too much hair on his legs, forgotten ear swab in his ear…

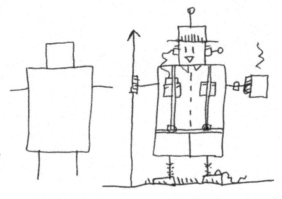

THE CRUEL DIVISOR

$$1 \; 2 \; 3 \; 4 \; 5 \; 6 \; 7 \; 8 \; 9 \; 10 \; 11 \; 12 \; 13 \; 14 \; 15$$

PLAYER	DIVISOR
$15 + 14 + 8 + 12$	$(1+3+5)(2+7)(4)(6)$
$= 49$	$= 28 + 9 + 10 + 11 + 13 = 71$

$$1 \; 2 \; 3 \; 4 \; 5 \; 6 \; 7 \; 8 \; 9 \; 10 \; 11 \; 12 \; 13 \; 14 \; 15$$

$13 + 9 + 15 + 6 + 14 + 8 + 12$ $(1) \; (3)(5)(2)(7)(4)$
$= 77$ $(6) = 28 + 10 + 11 = 49$

THIS SOLO GAME IS, BY EXCEPTION, NOT MY INVENTION. It is more than a century old, and its origin is unknown. Yet it is too original not to include it. First, write the numbers 1 to 15 (it can be made longer). See example. You got a Player and the Divisor. Player chooses a number and adds it to his score. However, the Divisor gets the digits (if still available) that divide that number evenly. He MUST get at least one divisor.

For example, if you choose 13, the Divisor gets the 1. If you then choose 15, the Divisor gets 5 and 3, but not the 1 anymore. BUT the Player also can't take the 3, 5, 7, or 11, since the Divisor MUST at least get one digit, and the 1 is already out of the game. Finally, if you can't play anymore, the Cruel Divisor gets all the remaining digits.

The winner is the one with the highest score. SEE EXAMPLE. Here we played two games. The little stripes above the numbers indicate that these are taken. The Divisor gets all the dividers plus the free numbers.

119 UPFOLDS

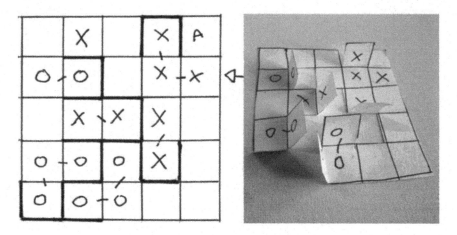

WE PLAY HERE (FOR CLARITY) ON A 5 X 5 GRID. A bigger field is however better. In turns both players place a mark on the board (X and O). When two of your marks are adjacent, you may fold one up. You do that by cutting three lines, as per the example.

The little lines mark the folds. In an abstract game, make the cut lines clear with a thick marker. In this game O reached 5 squares upwards, and X only 3. Moreover, in his last move, X placed his mark where the arrow points, and then tried to cut the lines and fold it upwards. Thus cutting off square A. But cutting off pieces or dividing the board in two is strictly forbidden. So X loses the game immediately.

The game becomes less abstract and easier when you really cut out the squares and physically fold them upwards.

COMBISQUARE

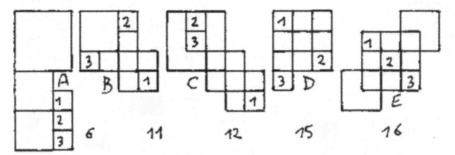

PUZZLE GAME. On squared paper, you put 6 squares: 1 of 3/3, 2 of 2/2 and 3 of 1: Example A. The goal is to form as many extra squares as possible.

Example B: one of the 2/2 squares is drawn in the big 3/3 (top left). The other 2/2 is drawn right below, with 1 common square. The 3 single squares are numbered for clarity. Result: 11 squares.

Example C: 12 squares.

Example D: 15 squares.

Example E: 16.

Puzzle: can you make a higher number than 16, and can you create all the other numbers from 6 to 16?

121 **POINT FIGURES**

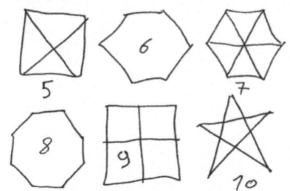

HERE WE SEE GEOMETRICAL FIGURES who have 5 to 10 points. Can you complete this series to 20? The figures need to be as simple and elegant as possible.

WE PLAY ON A 4 X 4 GRID. IN TURN, Circled and blank place digits 1-8 on the field until the 16 squares are full. Now equal numbers are crossed out, starting with 1, then 2, and so on until the grid is in 2 parts. You have to imagine that these squares are being "cut out." Do this until you can cut a whole piece, consisting of MORE than one digit, out of the paper.

The SMALLEST pieces are then thrown away. The remaining numbers of the opponents are counted. Winner is the one with the highest number.

EXAMPLE. After crossing out both digits 2, the digit 4 to the left has been cut out. But one number alone doesn't count. However, after crossing out both numbers 3 the paper is cut in two.

On top: 4558 and below: 66778. 4558 is thrown away. We only keep 66778. And there, it's clear that Blank 8 will win.

A   B   C

2→	↑ˣ		
		↑₄	
↓ˣ		↑₃	
↑₁			

⇱	←	→	⇡
↑	↑	⇡	←
↓	⇴	⇵	⇵
⇴	⇡	↓	↑

↓	↑	⇴	⇡
⇡	↓	↑	↑
↑	⇡	⇵	↓
⇵	←	↑	↓

VERY FAST LITTLE PASTIME GAME.
We play on 4 by 4. Players face each other, and try to draw as many arrows as possible in their direction. You may however also draw arrows in a different direction. If an arrow points at an adjacent square where another arrow points in a different direction, that arrow is destroyed.

See example A. Arrow 1 destroys arrow X. The same with arrow 2: X is destroyed. Arrow 3 however will not destroy 4: both in the same direction. You play until the board is full.

Winner is of course the one with the most arrows pointing in his direction.

Example B: arrow Up gets 3, Down 2.
Example C: Up 5, Down 4.

124 **CROSS DIVIDE**

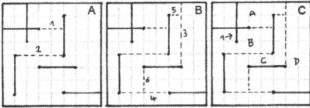

PUZZLE SOLO GAME TO BE PLAYED ON 8 X 8 SQUARED PAPER. First, draw somewhere in the field 6 lines of 3 squares long, 3 horizontal and 3 vertical. Then extend the endpoints freely until they collide with another line. You may lengthen the endpoints in any of the possible 3 directions. Or choose not to do that.

The goal is to make areas bordered by more than 4 lines. A. Line 2 is stopped

by another endpoint. B. Lines 5 and 6 are stopped by a previously drawn line. C. Area A: 6 border lines. B: 8 lines. The small line (1) does not count as a border line (and that point was not extended). C: 8 lines. D: 6 lines.

Is it possible to divide the square such that all areas count more than 4 border lines? And which is the highest number of border lines you can create?

	9 ⃰	10	11
8̶	2 •	1̶2̶	3̶
7̶	1	4 •	13 •
6	5	1̶4̶	

	12 •	1̶3̶ •	6
3 •	2̶	1	7
4̶	5	9̶	14 •
11	10	8 •	

TWO PLAYERS DRAW A FIELD OF 4 X 4 SQUARES. They write down the digits 1 to 14 in the squares. But they leave the top left square and the one below right, empty - see the example.

Players don't see each other's papers though. Then, in turn, they call a chosen number that is adjacent to an empty square. There are six of them. The opponent has to cross out that number wherever it stands on his board. If that happens to be adjacent to an empty square, he can't call that digit anymore.

SEE EXAMPLE. Left and right square (two opponents): digits with a point have been called. They are destroyed on the opponents' board. Winner is the one with the highest sum left. Right has 71 and Left 77. (Don't count it, just strike out equal numbers, and then you'll see it immediately).

X^1	X^1	X^1	1	^6O
2	$_3X$	^2O	3	^6O
$_4O$	$_3X$	^2O	^2O	^6O
$_4O$	$_3X$	X^5	X^5	X^5
$_4O$	X^7	X^7	X^7	4

O_3	O_3	O_1	X_6	1
O_7	O_3	O_1	X^6	X^6
O^7	X^2	O_1	X^4	^4X
O^7	X^2	X^2	X^4	X^8
O^5	O^5	O^5	X^8	X^8

WE PLAY ON A 5 X 5 GRID. Players place, in turn, each time THREE marks on the board. They must be in straight contiguous squares, in the form of a row, or a "hook."

See examples: the moves are numbered 1 to 8. However, in the first example, after 7, there is no place anymore for a move of contiguous three squares. So ALL the remaining, "open" squares go to the second player. Thus, in the first game, X reaches 12, and O gets 9 plus the four empty squares, so 13 in all. It's clear that the first player will always lose. However, the point is, by how much? So this game is all about these empty leftover spaces.

This means that, in fact, O gets 4 points. The game must be played twice, with the first player becoming the second. In the second game, O started, and X wins with only 1 empty square. So, final score: O gets 4, and X gets 1.

PAPER CHAMELEON

THE DESIGN IS RATHER CLEAR. The tail needs to be curled with a dull knife. Solid lines need to be cut, dashed lines need to be creased before folding. The tail has an open space. The legs also. For strength, the legs are doubled, and the feet should be separated.

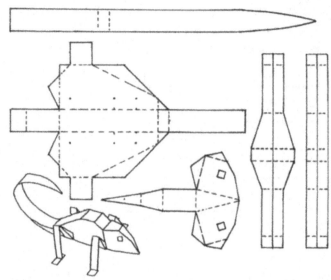

PAPER VEHICLES

PASTIME TINKERING. How to make the wheel for number one was already explained. For number two just fit 6 triangles together to make a "Hexagon Wheel." (6 strokes of paper divided equally in 3, plus a flap.) It is fun and a puzzle to create original and "sculptural" cars and carts. They're also a bit mysterious and "artsy." Try to invent all kinds of new "wheels."

X	X	X	X	O	O
O	O	O	X	O	X
O	O	O	X	O	X
O	O	O	X	X	O
X	X	O	X	O	X
O	X	O	X	X	X

x	x
	x

X :-4-1

O :-2 -5

WE USE A 6 X 6 GRID. In turns the players each write a mark on the field (or two at the same time if you want to be faster). But beforehand, out of sight of the opponent, they drew a "flap," a connected piece of paper consisting of 6 squares. See example at the right.

Now you must imagine that, at the end of the game, when the board is filled, you can connect this flap with the 6 x 6 field (at the outside). You then turn it so that it lies on the field. All the marks covered by that flap are dead.

You can use any side, and turn the flap, or even use the mirror image. Know that also YOUR OWN marks can be killed by your flap.

Plus, when the two flaps overlap, those marks are killed TWICE. In the example, this is the case with one X.

The winner is the one with the most remaining marks.

130 DICE TOPPLE

3	5 5	4 3
¹6	⁵1⁶	¹ 6 3
4³	5⁵	⁴2

1 - 5 - 4 - 1 - 3 - 5 - 4
- 1 - 5 - 6 - 3 - 5 - 4
- 6 - 3 - 5 - 6 - 3 - 2

TAKE A DIE. THEN DRAW 9 SQUARES JUST BIG ENOUGH TO FIT THE DICE INTO. Then imagine that you can "imprint" the digit onto the paper.

You can topple the dice in 4 (middle), or 3, or 2 directions. You cannot turn the dice inside a square. But you can choose which digit you want to imprint.

So, if you want for instance a 6 and you got a 5, you can ignore the 5 and topple the dice again, until you got your 5. Now, can I put all 6 numbers in all of the 9 squares? Yes! See example.

The small digits above the larger ones are numbers that we didn't want. To the right, we see the sequence of the turning dice. The underlined digits are the ones we chose to imprint.

131 FIVE FINGERS

DEXTERITY BRAIN GAME. Try to master this "five fingers technique" in case the Great Rubber Band War breaks out, and you get involved. If that happens, you will be powerless against the superior tactics of your opponents who could even shoot with two hands simultaneously.

That's EIGHT rubber bands flying in YOUR direction.

132 BUBBLE SLIME SWAMP ALIENS

DRAWING GAME. Even if you can't draw (or THINK you can't), creating simple figures can be very powerful. "Bubble slime swamp aliens armed with poisonous spears." Drawing is certainly also a "Brain Game."

WAVE OBJECT

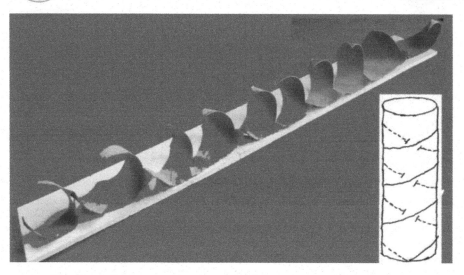

TINKERING GAME. "Random architecture," "random art"…

Use a cardboard kitchen paper roll. First cut along the solid line. Then start again along the dotted line.

But don't cut through the solid line. The lines should of course be drawn beforehand.

134 QUADRA

WE PLAY ON A 10 X 10 FIELD ON SQUARED PAPER. In turn, each player sets his mark. The goal is to create squares. See Example 1 (shown on 5 x 5). Circle managed to make one. He is allowed to fill it with circles (here only 1). But then (Example 2) Cross managed to make a big one. Again he fills it with crosses. And all enemy circles inside that square are destroyed, EXCEPT however those who were already in a square. They are protected. Even if it is only a small one of 2 by 2. See Example 3. Squares may also be diagonal.

The winner is the one with the most marks.

135 WHEEL OBJECT

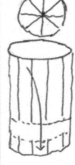

TAKE A CARDBOARD ROLL, make incisions along the vertical lines. Then glue the long ends to the flaps, but always take the next one. Use a circle divided in 8 to mark the vertical lines.

Make 4 of them and fix them to a cardboard car.

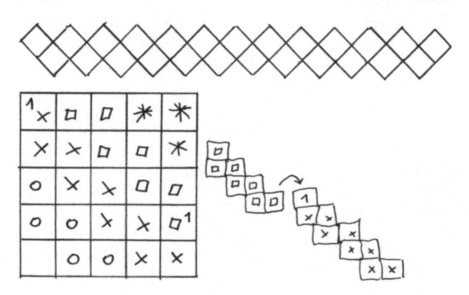

DRAW A SQUARE OF 5 X 5. IT CONTAINS 25 SQUARES. Theoretically, they can be used to make this long ladder on top. But in practice, we'll have to mark them up, use scissors, cut the pieces out, and even glue them together.

How high can this ladder become? And with a bigger square than 5 x 5?

In this example, the 1 of the square marks will need to be glued at the back of the 1 of the crosses. The figure of the squares must be reversed. And then you can add the stars and the circles.

| 2 | 2 | | 4 | → | 2 | 2 | | 4 | | 2 | 4 | 2 | 2 | 8 | 12 |

2	4	2	2	8	12
6	2	2	2	4	10
6	2	2	2	4	10
12	2	2	6	8	26
12	2	8	6	8	34

| 2 | 2 | 2 | | 6 | → | 2 | 2 | 4 | 4 | | → |

| 2 | 2 | 2 | 6 | 6 | → | 2 | 2 | 4 | 4 | 8 | → |

SOLITAIRE GAME. We play on a 5 by 5 field. First you put two neighboring numbers 2 somewhere. Then, successively, you play TWO moves each time. First you add EQUAL numbers (free choice, wherever on the board). You put the new number at the edge of the board, or against another number that blocks the road. See examples.

Next you put somewhere a new digit 2. You play on until the board is full. Only digits higher than 2 count for the final score!

138 HORRENDOUS CHAIR

TRY, AMONG FRIENDS, TO MAKE THE "UGLIEST CHAIR". Use light cardboard, scissors, glue, tape, tissue paper, thin ropes, staples, fibers, dust, banana peels... The majority decides which chair is the worst.

If no decision can be reached, use the scissors to defend your point of view.

(Humor and fun are also "Brain Games.")

139 ADDING MACHINE

7	11	5	3	9
6	4	2	6	8
4	1	3	9	11
16	9	7	15	19
11	16	13	24	37

PLACE THE DIGITS 1 TO 4 IN THE "MIDDLE" OF A 5 X 5 BOARD. They must be in a 2 x 2 space. (That space has 4 options: 1 or 2 rows above, and 1 or 2 columns to the left.) From then on add the digits up, straight or diagonally, placing the answer in any adjacent square.

It's very simple, see the example. Go for the highest number, here: 37.

Or for the highest total sum (you'll need a calculator).

It can be played solo, or as a contest with each player on his own board.

140 CRACKED STICKS FIGURES

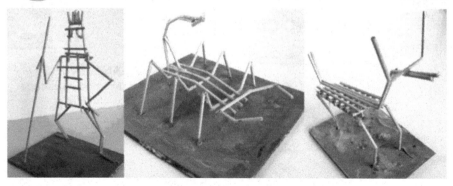

ALWAYS BREAK THE WOODEN STICKS HALF THROUGH, so that they are still connected. Then drop some glue in these joints.

Finally glue the whole thing together. Hiker in the woods (should have been made with real twigs and branches), a scorpion and a deer.

LUCKY COUNT

2	8 ˣ	3 ˣ	4
1 ˣ	7 •	9 •	8 ˣ
3 ˣ	4 •	7 ˣ	2
9 •	2	3 •	7 •

```
 •        ˣ
16       15
13       11
10        4  +2 +4 +2 +2
____     ____
39        40
```

MORE OF A GAME OF LUCK, BUT STILL FUN. The two opponents write down two four-digit numbers on a piece of paper. These numbers cannot contain zero, or two equal digits. Then they write them down on this board, in two turns. Here: 2834, 1798, 3472, 9237.

Next, they may claim two neighboring digits, straight or diagonal, and add them up. See the score of Dot and Cross to the right. Since the first player, Dot, has a slight advantage, Cross gets all the (isolated) digits that are not used, as an extra. Here 2, 4, 2, and 2. He wins.

LOOPS AND CIRCLES MAN

DRAWING GAME. Try to draw a figure or a face or a landscape with only loops and circles.

```
  A                              B                           C
 7 3 4 1    7+3+4+1=15         9 3 2 9   9+3+2+9=23        9 3 2 9
-1          1+5 =6             -9 ⤶      2+3 =5            + 2
 6 3 4 1                        0 3 2 9                     9 5 2 9
-4                              - 3                         - 3
 2 3 4 1                        0 3 2 6                     9 2 2 9
- 3         WAL2515            - 2                         -9 ⤶
 2 3 1 1                        0 3 2 4                     0 2 2 9
+ 7                            +9                           - 9
23 8 1      2+3+8+1= 14        9 3 2 4  9+3+2+4=18          0 2 2 0
            1+4= 5                      1+8= 9              = 4
```

SOLITAIRE GAME. WRITE A RANDOM NUMBER OF 4 DIGITS. Add the digits up, and the resulting digits again. Call this your "root number," See A. Now add OR subtract EACH of the ORIGINAL 4 digits from any one digit of the original (and then new) number. But you may not subtract a number from itself. See A: you cannot subtract the 7 from the 7, to reach zero.

But, see B and C: you may subtract the OTHER 9 from 9. Also, you are not allowed to make a decimal. You may however reach zero (but not 10). The result is a new number. Now with the same method take his "root." The goal is to finish with a lower root number than your opening number.

EXAMPLE A: last sum: 7 cannot be subtracted from 2 or 3 or 1. It must be added then, but not at 3 since this will give 10, which is not allowed. (If blocked, you lose the game.) The new root is 5, so less than 6.

EXAMPLE B: the new root is 9, so the game is lost.

EXAMPLE C: this variation is better!

TRY OUT RANDOM DESIGNS AND TEMPLATES with light cardboard. Let chance decide what the result will be: a car, an alien, a geometrical object, an abstract sculpture, or some kind of "new" animal?

(145) **STUFFED STAPLES**

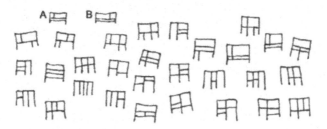

PASTIME DOODLE GAME. Always start from a rectangle (staple shape), with an open bottom. Then draw 3 straight lines. Try to get as many "types" of the figure as possible. Types are different, where the shape is different, not the exact position of the lines. For example figure A equals figure B.

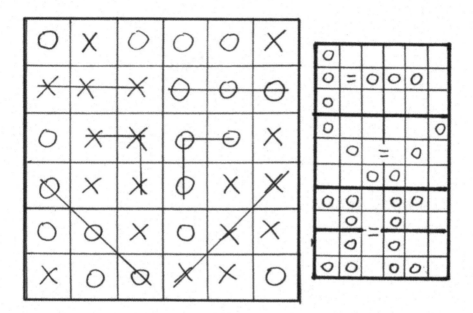

WE PLAY ON A GRID, 6 X 6. In turns Cross and Circle set their marks wherever they want on the field. After that, equal series of three marks (of Cross AND Circle) are crossed out simultaneously.

he winner is the one who has the most series of three marks left, or else, a series of only two marks. In this example, O has 1 of 3 marks, and 1 of 2. And Cross has only 3 of 2 marks. O wins, since a series of 3 marks is more important. See example to the right.

An equal series of three marks are 3 in a column that equals 3 in a row. Or three diagonal slanting to the right or to the left. Or three in a "hook"– so 4 variations.

PASTIME DOODLE GAMES.

1. Draw 20 short horizontal lines. Close your eyes. Draw 10 vertical lines, and try to cross out as many horizontal lines as you can.

2. Draw 10 rectangles. Close your eyes. Try to draw 10 crosses in the middle of these squares.

3. Draw 10 circles. Close your eyes. Try to draw 2 roads between these circles.

148 **PREMISE FINDER**

WORD GAME. "I WENT TO THE ZOO, BUT IT WAS RAINING. LUCKILY I BROUGHT MY COAT."

From this we can conclude:
1. Sometimes he goes to the zoo. 2. He doesn't like rain. 3. Sometimes it rains. 4. He can walk. 5. The zoo is sometimes open. 6. Sometimes he is lucky. 7. He has a coat. 8. Sometimes he brings his coat. 9. His coat helps against the rain. 10. He has enough money to pay the entrance fee. 11. He survived his trip to the zoo, since he speaks in the past. 12. He knows the way to the zoo. 13. He can feel rain...

This can be played with multiple players, each making a valid statement, in a rapid succession - perhaps the most premises discovered wins.

3 1 4 9 6 2 3 5 3	6 8 9 3 9 2 1 6 6	1 7 4 9 5 6 3 5 4	3 5 7 4 9 2 2 3 5
3 1 4 9 6 +5 +3 +2 +3	6 8 9 3 9 +2 -1 +6 +6	1 7 4 9 5 -6 -3 -5 -4	3 5 7 4 9 -2 +2 +3 -5
8 4 6 9 9 4 2 3 0	8 8 8 9 15 1 8 4	1 1 1 4 1 3	1 7 7 7 4 6 3
8 4 6 9 9 +2 +4 +3	8 8 8 9 1 5 -1 +8 -4	1 1 1 4 1 -3	1 7 7 7 4 +6 +3
10 8 9 9 9 7 1	8 8 8 8 9 1 1 8	1 1 1 1 1	7 7 7 7 7
10 8 9 9 9 +7 +1	8 8 8 8 9 1 -1 +8		
8 9 9 9 9 1	8 8 8 8 8 9 1		
+1 9 9 9 9	8 8 8 8 8 9 -1		
9 9 9 9 9	8 8 8 8 8 8		

SOLITAIRE GAME. We write down a random number. Then we calculate the difference between the digits. These we can add or subtract from any digit we want. See example. However we have to use all four of them and only once. All zeros fall away.

The goal is to reach equal numbers with zero difference.

THE CAT WANTS TO EXPLORE THIS CUBE BUILDING. There are only 5 entrances (circles). In the interior, all cubes are connected with circle openings, including the ceiling and the floor.

How many cubes will she have to pass through? Knowing that going IN a cube and then coming OUT again counts for TWO cubes. And where will the cat best enter the building? Of course, she will try to achieve the shortest way.

As a variation, you can allow her to go outside and then back in again through another door. We give a simple example, but much more complicated mazes can be designed. And of course, THAT is the real puzzle here.

151 LIFELINE

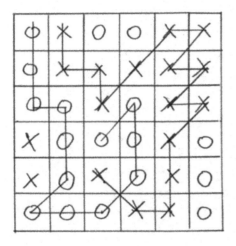

IN TURN, PLAYERS WRITE DOWN TWO MARKS in a grid of 6 x 6. When the board is full, they try to connect their marks, straight or diagonal, into 1 long, continuous line.

Here O reaches 13, and X reaches 16. Obviously, X won.

152 BLOCK BATTLE

DRAW A 6 X 6 FIELD. Each player has blocks of 3 squares and blocks of 2 squares. But one has to lay them horizontally, and her opponent vertically. Each mark on the grid is awarded a point.

SEE EXAMPLE: the situation after 5 moves each. Each player has 5 rows of three, which is 15 points. However, X can place a vertical block of two on A and B. So he gets 4 points extra, and wins.

O	O	O	O	O	O
O	O	O	X	X	B
	X	A	X	X	B
X	X	A	X	X	X
X	X	O	O	O	X
X		O	O	O	X

153 DOZENPOINT

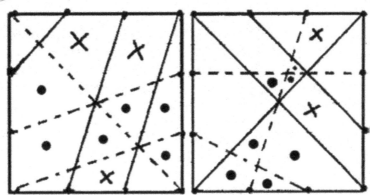

WE PLAY ON A SQUARE WITH EACH SIDE DIVIDED INTO THREE BY TWO equally spaced points. Two colors are needed, here represented by a solid line and a dashed one. In turn players connect 2 points with a ruler. A point may only be used once. The goal is to create areas bordered by a majority of your color, each of which scores a point. The borders of the square don't count.

EXAMPLE: the surfaces of Dashed Line are marked with a black dot. Solid Line with an X. A surface with equal borderlines is a draw.

154 SENTENCE ASCENSION

"I VISITED BARCELONA AND WENT TO THE CATHEDRAL." Now define a higher set for each word. I = person. Visited = moving. Barcelona = city. And = connection. Went = walking. To = direction. The = pointing. Cathedral = building. So: "Person moving city connection walking direction pointing building." And then translate that again as you like: "She swam Mont Saint Michel plus ran through their monastery."

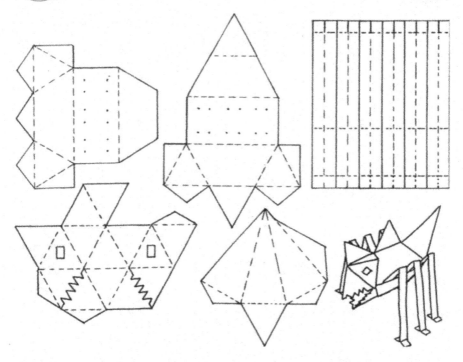

ALL SOLID LINES NEED TO BE CUT, all dashed lines to be creased and folded.

The body has two parts. The tail is three dimensional. There is a dorsal fin. The legs are double for strength. The feet need to be separated. The head is a bit of a puzzle, but you'll figure it out.

156 CUBES ARE ALIVE

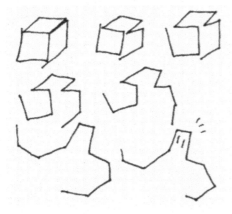

SEE THE TRANSFORMATION OF A CUBE into a living person.

So…what else can a Cube become? You are allowed to draw eyes.

157 16-PAGE BOOKLET

TEMPLATE for a 16 page little notebook, or magazine.

158 RHYME CRIME TIME

WORD GAME. TAKE A RANDOM SENTENCE: "I walked in the rain with my boots." Then find a rhyme for each word: "Spy blocked spin a plane myth fly routes." (Feel free to use an online rhyme dictionary.)

Now explain the new sentence: "The foreign agent stopped the mythical plane to fly his normal routes by giving it a spin."

159 ONE TWO THREE

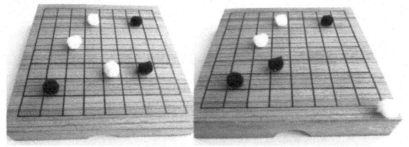

A			3		
			2		
	3	2	1	2	
		1	O	3	
			1	2	3

A FAST STRATEGIC BOARD GAME. Black and white start with 3 balls in opposite corners. From there the balls MUST move 3 squares, but in straight lines only. See first image: some possible moves of the ball in the middle.

Now look at the boards. This is the situation. Now black jumps ON and OVER white and removes it from the board. And since it is also allowed to strike in a series, as in Checkers/Draughts, Black jumps ON two other White balls and wins.

160 EXTRACTOR

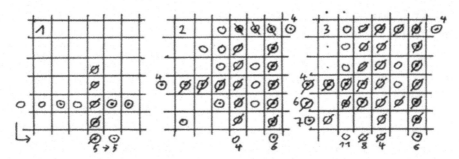

EACH PLAYER PUTS 6 MARKS ON THIS 6 X 6 GRID. (Here we use Circle and Circle with a dot.) From then on they may move 1 square further. But they may also go out of the board. If that happens, they will "suck up" the whole row or column. If they swallow for instance 3 marks, they get "Power 4," including the "Attractor" itself. These outside Attractors may move along the borders, unless they meet an obstacle. Important: moving Attractors MUST CROSS OUT their former position. But the marks on the board do NOT.

Example 1. Attractor O can swallow 5 marks, and gets "Power 6." He can try to swallow enemy Attractor O dot 5. But O dot creates a barrier, and swallows an extra mark.

Example 2. (New game). O dot made Attractor 6, and O made O 4. O now cannot make a new Attractor between these two, since that would be swallowed immediately by O dot 6. So O 4 goes to the left, and swallows 4 more marks.

Example 3. Endgame. O 11 can swallow O dot 7. O dot 6 can grow to 8. O can make more marks top left on the board, swallow them and merge two Attractors power 4 and reach 8. O dot 4 can't do anything since it would take too many moves, and Attractors of the same value can't swallow each other anyway. Final result: O: 11+7+4+4=26. O dot: 6+2+4=12.

161 THE THREE-STICK BOW

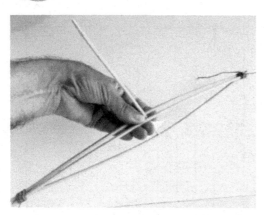

USE LONG WOODEN STICKS.
Bind three together, and use the flexibility of the wood itself to create tension for the bow. Can be useful for "survival" if you lack string long enough to be used as a bowstring. Fire away from people!

162 MEANING CLEANING

PASTIME WORD GAME. Take a sentence: "I was fired because my boss told me I was lazy."

Now transform that sentence completely, but still try to keep the original meaning. BUT you have to use every original word. "Was fired my lazy me because boss told I was I."

"The sea was too cold so we went back to the hotel." Transformation: "Too cold the sea back the hotel to was so we went."

163 LABRAT

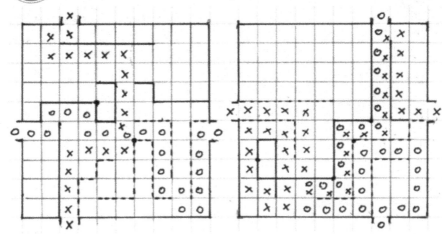

WE PLAY ON A GRID 10 BY 10. We should use colors - but here X and O. X chooses 2 gates, facing each other, and O does also, but in a different *direction. See example.* Then in turn, X and O draw 5 barriers of 5 continuous lines. Barriers may cross each other. It is forbidden to close the gateways completely. Finally X and O connect their gates.

The one who can do that in the least squares, wins.

164 EIGHT LINES TRIANGLE

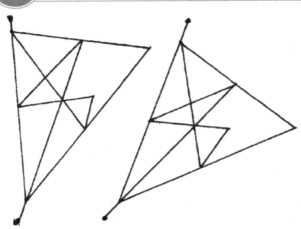

DRAWING GAME. Try to draw this continuous line doodle freehand, very fast and accurately.

1	2	3
4	5	6
1	2	3
4	5	6

$6 \times 10 = 60$	$3 \times 10 = 30$
$2 \times 10 = 80$	$3 \times 10 = 60$
$5 \quad = 85$	$6 \quad = 66$
$5 \quad = 90$	$1 \times 10 = 76$
$4 \quad = 94$	$1 \times 10 = 86$
$4 \quad = 98$	$2 \quad = 88$

IN TURN, A PLAYER CAN TAKE ONE NUMBER OUT OF THIS BOARD, see example. He may use it as it is, or multiply it by 10. Players must play 6 times. Mark the digits that you took out. The goal is to reach 100, or be as close as possible. But if you go over 100, you lose immediately.

SEE EXAMPLE. Next to the board are the moves of the two players. Left was a bit aggressive, but it worked out, while Right was a bit too prudent.

166 DOUBLE PLUS DOMINO

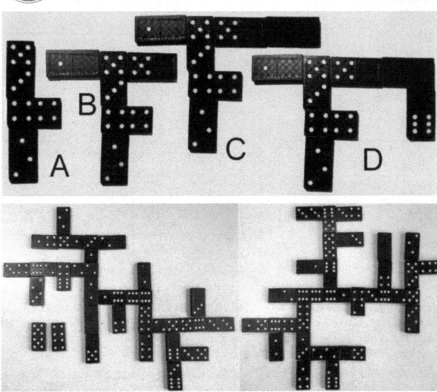

EXAMPLE A: WE START WITH A 4-4 DOMINO. Against it, we lay a 1 and a 3 = 4. B: we surround the 5 with a 5 and a zero = 5. C: against that zero we place another zero. That is, as an exception, allowed without placing a second zero. D: and on that zero another zero. And so on.

The goal is to try to find a place for ALL the stones. See the finished games underneath. Number one was not successful.

167 PSYCHIC

INSPIRED BY THE GAME "PROPHECIES" BY ANDY JUELL (WITH CHANGED RULES). The goal is to PREDICT how many numbers will be in a row, column, or diagonal. In turn, players place their number (here blank and underlined), on a 4 x 4 grid. But instead of doing that, they can also put a cross in a square. See example 1. After blank 4, underlined 3 sets a cross above that 4. Thus making the 4 UNTRUE, and increasing the chances of underlined 3. In the end, blank wins the game.

The score to the right indicates the digits that are TRUE.

For example: for the upper row one 3 and two underlined 3's are correct and give the exact number of digits in that row, which is 3.

168 SIMPLISTIC PORTRAITS

TRY TO DRAW EXTREMELY SIMPLE PORTRAITS of your friends, sitting around the table.

But first, try it out yourself before the mirror.

169 MULTIPLUS

[Four example 5×5 grids showing the Multiplus game progression:]

Grid 1: 11 | 1 | 2 | | ; 10 | | 3 | 4 | ; | 9 | 6 | 5 | ; | 7 | 8 | |

Grid 2: 10 | 1 | 2 | | ; 9 | 11 | | 3 | 4 ; | 8 | 6 | 5 | ; | 7 | | |

Grid 3: | | 8 | 6 | 4 ; 9 | 7 | 5 | 3 | ; 10 | 1 | 2 | | ; 11 | | | |

Grid 4: | | | | ; | | | | ; | | 4 | 3 | ; 5 | 6 | 1 | 2 ; 7 | 8 | |

SOLITAIRE GAME. FIRST DRAW A BOARD 5 BY 5 SQUARES.

Then put number 1 somewhere. Now uneven numbers move with a STRAIGHT line to the next higher number, while even ones do that with a DIAGONAL line.

See examples. You have won when you can connect 11 (in a straight line since 11 is an uneven number) with 1. In the last example we are blocked, since 8 is even, and there is no place for a diagonal connection.

170 EIGHT SPLIT

[Two 4×4 grids, each showing an example of splitting into two sets of 8 squares with a bold dividing line.]

TWO OPPONENTS TRY TO FIND EACH AS MANY WAYS as possible to split a 4 x 4 grid into two (i.e. 2 lots of 8 squares). Mirror images also count.

Who finishes first, wins. Here are two examples.

SEE EXAMPLE ABOVE. FIRST WE LAY TWO STONES TOGETHER. Here: 6/6 and 1/5. Then we look for a stone that fits on top in the middle: stone 6/1. Second row on top: we build further by laying a 5/3 and a 2/2 against the group. A 3/6 and a 2/5 can be put over it. This way we build onward.

The goal is to include all of the stones in the castle, and to build it as high as possible. See example: we are left with two stones we can't place, and we only reached level two.

172 NINEX

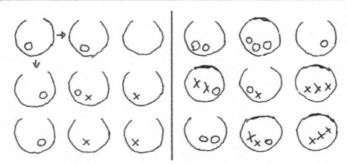

WE START BY DRAWING 9 OPEN CIRCLES. Circle puts one mark top left and Cross bottom right. From there they may jump in a straight line in 4 directions to an adjacent OPEN circle. Once a circle is occupied by 3 marks, it is closed. You cannot jump any more from, or to it.

The goal is to create as many marks as possible. However only the ones in a CLOSED circle are counted. The others are lost. If one player is blocked, the other may go on. Playing is not mandatory, but when the two players pass, the game is over.

See example: Circle has 5 points and Cross 10.

173 NINE SPLIT

THIS LOOKS LIKE ANOTHER GAME "EIGHT SPLIT" but is more difficult.

Prepare 2 empty, 6 x 6 grids. Now opponents get 3 minutes to draw "divisions of 9." So 9 squares that form a connected region (straight, not diagonal).

SEE EXAMPLE. The one who finishes the most (correctly and differently from each other) in 3 minutes wins.

WE DRAW 10 BOARDS OF 4 X 4 FREEHAND. Now you have to imagine that O and X each have two "bars" of two squares. One is vertical, the other horizontal. See starting position top left. They may, with each move, slide one of their bars. Moving is obligatory. When you're blocked, you lose. It is forbidden to reverse your previous move. If there is no other possibility, then again, you're blocked, and you lose.

EXAMPLES:

See board 6: O cannot move again to A, since that was his previous move.

Last field: O and X can claim all the squares where they, hypothetically, could be moving in with a next move. A is for X, B is for O. X has five, O has two, and both have 1 in common. So X wins.

175 ARTIST BOOK

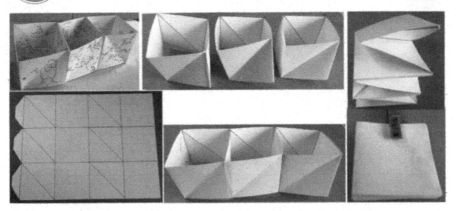

SMALL NOTEBOOK OR ARTIST BOOK. Can be a sculptural object as well as a flat book. You can add as many elements as you like. Make sure that the flaps are hidden between two glued together. This way you have 8 outside pages and 12 inside pages to write on. To close the book you have to twist it.

176 EXPLODING CUBE

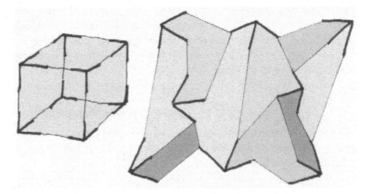

DOODLE GAME. A cube has 8 corners where 3 lines come together. Now draw them separately and randomly. Then try to connect the lines to create a more or less possible geometric figure. This attempt clearly failed.

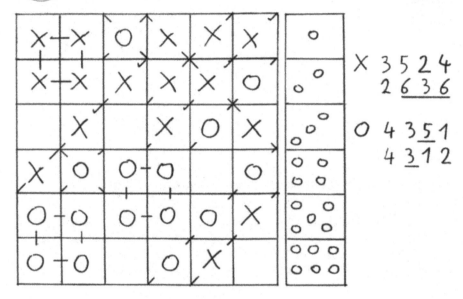

WE PLAY ON A 6 X 6 GRID. In turns opponents throw a die and then they write the outcome on the field. However, this has to be done in the exact way as the digits are usually noted on the dice itself. See example to the right.

This is of course a game of luck. Nevertheless, some tactics can be useful. For instance, if you throw a five, you can put that number so that it becomes difficult for the opponent to write down another big number. When a player has no place to write his digit, he has to pass. Each player has 8 turns.

To the right, we see the sequence of X and O, representing their results of the dice rolls. The underlined numbers indicate that there was no place left for it on the board. X reaches 16 (total number) and O 15.

1 3		1 3	1̶ 3	1̶ 1̶	1̶ 1̶
1 4		1 4	1̶ 4	1 3	1 4
2		2	2		2 1 1

1̶ 3	1 1	1̶ 3	1̶ 1̶	1̶ 1̶ 1̶	1̶ 1̶
1̶ 4	1	1	1̶ 4̶	1̶ 3̶ 3	1̶ 4̶ 3̶
2		2 4	2̶ 1̶	2̶ 4 2	2̶ 1̶ 1
			2̶ 3	3̶ 1̶ 2	1 1 1
				4 1̶	

THIS IS AN ADAPTATION, WITH CHANGED RULES, OF THE GAME "PENNYWISE," played with real coins. See example.

At the top left is the starting situation. Each player has 5 "coins," two ones, 2, 3, and 4. By each move opponents are obliged to put at least one coin "on the table," They may however take "change" back, on the condition that it has to be a total of lower value. So, when you give a 4, you may take out 1,1,1, or 2,1, or 3.

See example: situation after the second move of Left. Right will now throw a 3 on the table and pull out 1 and 1. (But he could have also given a 2 and a 1, together 3).

The loser is the one who has no more coins.

Example below right: Left has to give his last 3. But since he started, Right must do one more gift. But he has four ones. (You can make this game more complicated by adding extra values, and create your own "paper coins", and playing it physically.)

X	O	O	X	O	X
X		X	X	O	O
O	O	X	O	X	O
X	O	O		O	
X		X		X	O
O	1	x	x	2	O

IN TURNS PLAYERS PUT DOWN THEIR MARK ON A 6 BY 6 FIELD.

The loser is the one who, inadvertently, makes 3 in a row (including diagonally).

But a player also loses if blocked, because they HAVE to make 3 in a row for their next move. This is the case for X in this example. O on the other hand can still make two moves: on 1 and 2.

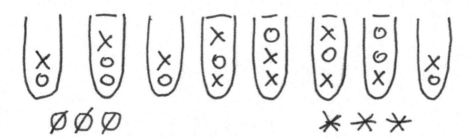

FIRST, WE DRAW 8 "PITS." Underneath, Circle and Cross have 3 marks. In turn, they may cross one out and put it in a pit. From there they may "jump" to an ADJACENT pit (and in a later move, even return).

When a pit is filled with 3 marks, it is closed. Playing is not obligated. Winner is the one with the most marks on top. Example: X = 6. O = 2.

WE PLAY ON A 6 X 6 GRID. In turns each opponent puts his mark on the paper. When that is done, we start to make "houses" with our own marks. Some templates will give you a "complete house,, with 4 walls and a roof.

The floor can be open, we tilt that to the bottom.

A house can also have 3 walls and even 2 (but it always needs a roof). A full house gives 6 points, with 3 walls is 3 points, and two walls is 1. See example.

O has 3 complete houses, making 18 points. The X has two 4-wall houses, 1 with 3, and 1 with 2. That totals 12 + 3 + 1 = 16.

This game can be a challenge for the imagination, but you can always cut the template out, and make the house.

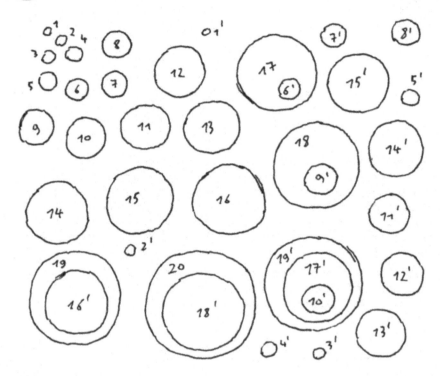

PASTIME DRAWING GAME. Draw freehand 20 circles that always grow bigger and bigger, and then smaller again.

183 SHOOTERS

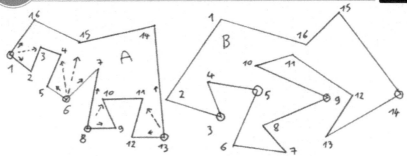

PUZZLE PASTIME. See "room" A. It has 16 corners. Now imagine that these are doors. Unwanted criminals can come through them. Luckily you have 4 guardsmen, armed with machine guns. How best to place them so that all corners are covered?

Guard 6 (circle) can shoot an intruder at 5, 4, 15, and 7 and guard 8 covers 7, 10, and 9. It's clear: terrorists can't enter here.

Problem: we WANT them to enter. Surprisingly, drawing a better room is not so easy. See B. Shooter 14 even covers corners (doors) 13, 12, 11, 16, and 15. Luckily, there is one door: 7, through which we (criminals) can enter without being shot.

So, let's try to draw some more rooms like that with even more "free doors."

184 TENSTAR

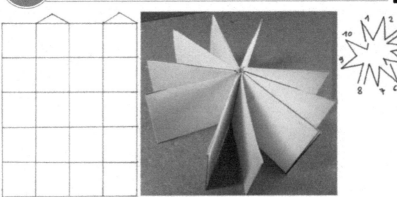

DESIGN FOR A SMALL NOTEBOOK. Also, a thin string can be placed in the middle to hang it as an artist booklet.

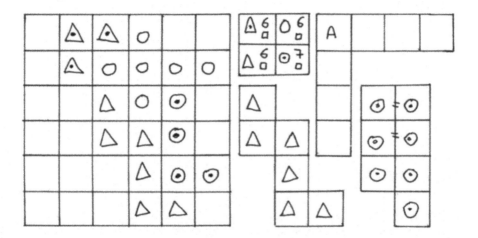

HERE WE TRY TO CREATE TEMPLATES TO MAKE A CUBE. Each opponent starts with 2 marks anywhere on this field (Circle White + Dot, Triangle White + Dot). With each move, players may add 1 other mark. However, these must be adjacent to your specific marks.

It is allowed to construct templates with double parts to reach the other side of the cube. See example A: under A you got the left side, then a double "roof," then the right side.

Once a cube is finished, or it becomes impossible to make one, you MUST STOP adding marks to that template.

Now look at the game: White Circle and White Triangle each finished 1 cube. While Triangle Dot and Circle Dot both will be able to make one, unimpeded by the opponent. So it's a draw.

However, Circle Dot needed 7 squares to make one, and when it's a draw, the winner is the one who needed the LEAST amount of squares. So Triangle wins.

See on the right side the templates for Triangle White and the (future) template for Circle Dot (the two stripes on the lines mean that they must be cut).

If in doubt, draw it, cut it out, test it. You should use a board of at least 10 x 10, and maybe more initial marks. You could also use several colors.

SET CROSS

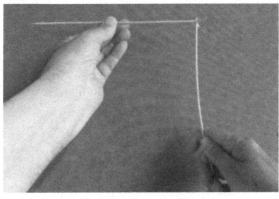

DRAW A BOARD 5 ON 5. Red and blue (here 1 and Roman 1) draw in turn each time a 1 and a minus one (-1) somewhere on the board. And so on. There are 25 squares, one will stay empty.

Now, in turn, players may cross out 2 digits: one of their own, and one enemy digit. However they have to stand next to each other. And their sum has to be zero: so a 1 versus a -1. Then all the digits are added up.

The player who achieved the highest positive number wins.

187 THE STICK BOW

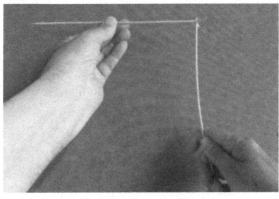

TAKE TWO WOODEN STICKS USED AS SKEWERS TO EAT OR BARBECUING. Any supermarket has them, and they are great tinkering material. Then split the "arrow" at the rear end. And use the flexibility of the other stick to create tension.

Now try to master the "Stick Bow," well away from other people.

OPEN TOWER

1		10			
2		11			
3	6	7	8	9	
4	X	12	X	18	
5 ⚡14	13	15	16	17	
	26	X	19		
22	23	24	20	25	
	27	X	21		
30	28	31	32	33	
	29	X	34		
38	39	40	35	41	
		36			
		37			

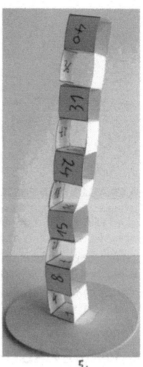

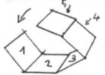

A CARDBOARD TOWER WITH SIDES THAT ARE ALTERNATELY OPEN,
out of 1 template. Can we build an infinite long tower out of 1 template? Yes.

First, cut out the outlines. Then crease all the lines with a dull knife. The lines with a double stripe on it must be cut. All the crossed-out squares also, but they can be reached by these double striped lines. So all can be done with small scissors. Then fold all the other lines.

See small drawing: fold 1 to 5 (numbers on the inside). Glue 5 on 1. Then glue 9 on the back of 3. From there on, you're on your own.

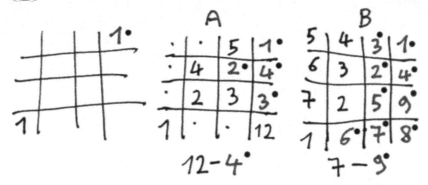

THIS IS A SMALLER AND FASTER VARIATION OF SEQUENTIUM. We play on 4 X 4 squares. Bottom left (perhaps blue) 1 starts, and top right (say red) 1 (here marked with a black dot). Both try to reach the highest possible number. Digits may move to an adjacent square, straight and diagonally.

Starting again from a lower digit like in Sequentium is now forbidden. If a number is blocked, the other may play on.

EXAMPLES: A. "Dot" is blocked with 4. "Blue" 4 may play on and can reach 12 (follow the points). B. Blue is blocked at 7. Red (dot) reaches 9.

190 **POCKET NOTEBOOK**

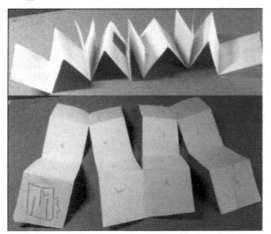

THIS IS THE WAY TO CUT A SHEET of paper and fold it into a small pocket notebook of 32 pages.

191 | DOMINO TRAIN

PUSH THE 0-0 DOMINO with another domino over the rails and through the tunnels. (Handiness is also a form of intelligence and thus a Brain Game.)

192 | DICE WISE

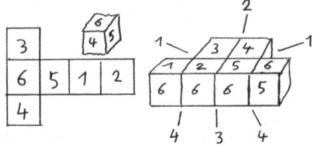

TAKE (OR MAKE) SIX DICE. We see the structure of a die to the left. All opposite numbers equal 7. This is the counter-clockwise arrangement, also known as "right-handed dice." This is common in the West, but in China, clockwise dice are used.

Now the puzzle is: can you put the dice in such a line that the digits 1 to 6 on top are aligned in a numerical order? (The line is allowed to bend at right angles.) Yes, there are several possibilities. Here we show one. Find all the others.

DESTRUCTOR DRONES

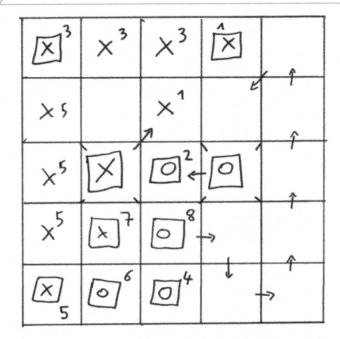

PLAYERS START ON A 5 X 5 BOARD with their mark (here outlined O and X) in the indicated positions (surrounded by four direction arrows). Next, the drones may move straight or diagonally to wherever they want. There they place a new mark. But everything in their path is destroyed.

However, it is also allowed NOT to destroy the intermediate squares. Marks are outlined circles and crosses. Simple circles and crosses are destroyed territory. The numbers indicate the successive moves. Destroyed or formerly occupied squares cannot be crossed or jumped over. SEE EXAMPLE.

O2 goes to O4 (move number 4), but does NOT destroy the square in between. Then O6, then X7, then O8. Now Cross is blocked. Since the winner is the one with the most destroyed territory (including former positions), O wins, since he can destroy the whole territory to the right (see arrows).

194 KILL THREE

1				2
	3			1
2	3			
	2		3	
1				

~~1~~			3	~~2~~
3	3	~~1~~	~~2~~	1
~~2~~	3		3	~~2~~
1	~~2~~	3	3	3
1	2	~~2~~		~~2~~

FIRST, IN TURNS, PLAYERS EACH PUT A DIGIT 3 ON A 5 X 5 GRID. After these two 3's the mark of player one is a 1, and player two a 2. Players put, in turns, their mark on the field.

But they are also allowed to write a number 3. Whenever a 1 or a 2 stands next to a 3, horizontally or vertically, the 1 or the 2 is destroyed.

Goal: To reach the highest number of your own marks. See example. After three turns, the 1 decided to put a 3 (underlined) between the two 2's, thus destroying them. Endgame in the example: three times 1 and only one 2. Player 1 won.

195 NOTEBOOKS LOOKS

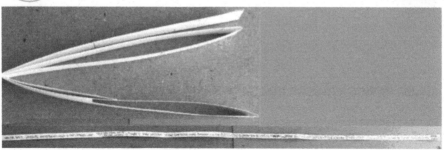

A VERY LONG THIN STRIP OF PAPER, just enough for one or two text lines has an amazing effect when you pull it out of your pocket, and unfold it. You can make it really VERY long and fold it. Easy to write and read. Can afterwards be shown as a work of art in a gallery…

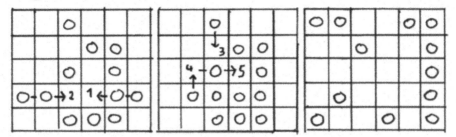

TWO PLAYERS EACH DRAW A GRID OF 6 X 5 SQUARES. In that, they write 12 marks, as spread out as possible. Now the opponent has to "order" the marks into one closed "block" of 4 by 3 marks. The marks may move 1 square, in all directions, also diagonally. They may also jump over another mark, even in a series if that is possible (this counts for 1 move).

The goal is to complete the block in as few moves as possible. See Example. Left: this was the beginning. 1 and 2 are jumps. Middle: Then 3, 4, and 5 make the block complete. Right: another, more complicated start. On this first try, the player needed 10 moves.

197 **DIGIT FILLER**

2	3
1	4	5
9	8	6	7
10	11	12	13	14

RULES: IN THIS REGULAR BOARD OF 14 SQUARES, a player has written down the number 1 in a random place. From there she has gone on to the next square, (horizontally, not diagonally, and then she has jumped over a former digit). See example.

All is well until 7. But the 7 may jump over the 6, and go on from there. Now each player draws an irregular board of 20 squares using digits. Then present the empty board to your opponent.

The goal is of course to fill the whole board.

SPIRAL NOTEBOOK

SMALL NOTEBOOK. The design is clear. When it finally comes out of your pocket, filled with shopping lists, ideas, drawings, doodles…it can be shown as a work of art.

MEMORY LINES

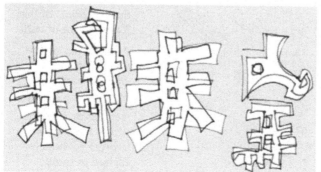

BLIND DOODLE GAME.
Draw abstract forms. Then close your eyes, and, with another color, try to outline them by memory.

YES WALKING
COMPUTER
FRIENDS JUNGLE
DEAD CRIMINAL CANOE
BANANA EXPLOSION

LANGUAGE GAME. Write down 10 words, but not too complicated ones. Give that to your opponent. You will get 10 in return.

Now stand up, read the words, and then start telling a story, as short as possible, where you use all ten words. The best story wins.

"YES, I was WALKING with my FRIENDS in the JUNGLE. But a CRIMINAL in a CANOE stole my BANANA. I hit him with my COMPUTER, but somehow there was an EXPLOSION in the machine and he was DEAD."

201 **THE TRIKE LEG HIKER**

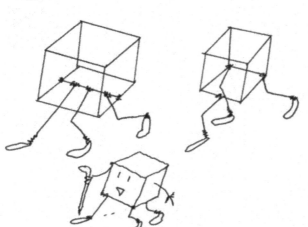

MAKE THIS IN IRON WIRE. Now study the walk of such a tripod creature. Draw the footprints of this 3-legged robot cube.

What would be the most efficient way to walk for him?

Then try it this way (second drawing) where the legs are not in one line, but attached to three different points.

202 TRIODROP

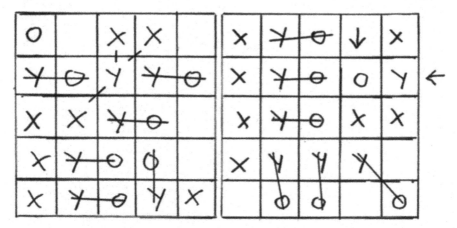

SOLO GAME. WE PLAY ON A 5 X 5 GRID. In turns, we put an X, a Y, and an O (simultaneously) on the field. These however have to be connected in 1 group, be it straight or diagonally (or both).

We go on until we can't place such a group anymore. At least one open space will remain. But the X cannot survive without a link with Y. While O can kill both X and Y, but only one of those at a time.

The goal is to leave as many Xs as possible.

See example.

After the marks are drawn, we do the settlement. Of course, we try to spare as much X as possible, and we mainly let O kill the Y. But bear in mind that X cannot survive without a Y as a neighbor.

In the first game, only three X fulfill that requirement. In the second game we have a choice: if we let O kill the Y, then the three X are lost. So we kill one X, and the other two have a Y as a neighbor and survive.

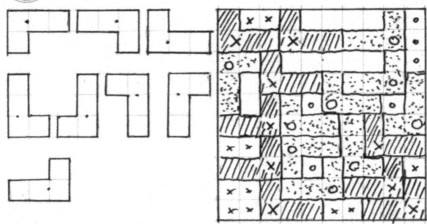

FIRST DRAW A BOARD OF 10 X 10. Now, in turn, blue and red may draw a shape of 4 squares (including an angle). Here, in black/white, represented by X and O. For clarity it's best to shade your tiles.

You play until there is no more place for another tile. The squares (in the holes) that are left become property of the color that has the most bordering lines. See example.

The owner of the "hole" gets 1 point per square. See example: 3 holes are a draw. X - 11, O – 6.

204 **HOLE BOXING**

THROW A PIECE OF CARDBOARD up in the air with a hole in it. And then try to SMASH your fist in that hole. Speed is the key. This must be a part of your daily Kung Fu training!

BOX DETECTOR

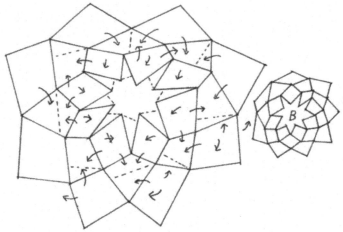

PASTIME DRAWING GAME. First, draw an 8-pointed star like in B, and then connect the endpoints, and again, and again. Then try to find "Boxes" with box lids. You may draw some dashed lines to clarify or create them.

You get 1 point for every box lid. I lost count here. Box lids and boxes may be seen from every angle, and then count double or triple.

CUBE MAZE

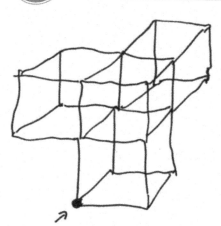

DRAW A FEW CUBES CONNECTED TO EACH OTHER. Then, with another color, try to trace as many sides of these cubes as possible.

You may of course not follow the same line twice. Do that as a contest: which one of the opponents will score the most sides? Also, try to add more cubes, or allow the players to double 1 line. Can you then cover all sides?

SEE EXAMPLE. Here we drew the skeleton of four cubes. Start at the indicated point (or wherever you want).

SQUAREGROW

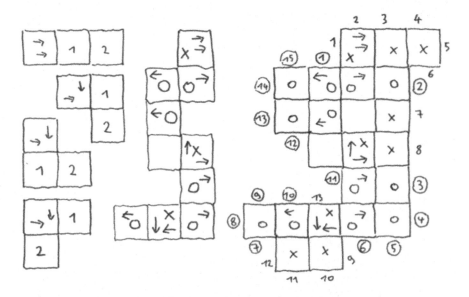

FIRST DRAW 10 NEIGHBORING SQUARES IN A RANDOM ORDER. Then, in turn, Cross and Circle may draw SIX arrows in these squares. And no more than TWO in one square. These arrows may point in any direction.

Then, in turn, players may "grow" to a neighboring square if they have an arrow in that direction. They may also, in a next turn, grow an additional square to their first one, if they have 2 arrows. The direction may be different, and they may choose which arrow to use first. See examples of possible moves.

Winner is the one who has the most outlines in the total figure (each side is 1 point). Circle reaches 15 and Cross only 13.

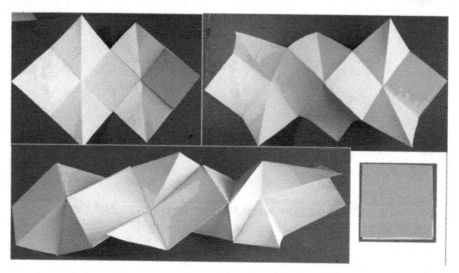

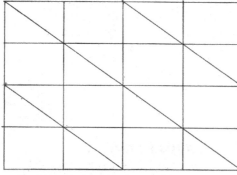

ON TOP LEFT: 2 STAR, 3 STAR... SQUARES.

You need to glue them together. They all fold to 1 square.

The template to the left, on top becomes the picture bottom left.

It does fold a bit strangely, as seen in the picture at the bottom.

But it has the advantage that you can use a full page for the template.

With a bigger cardboard cover front and back this is easily solved. Of course, we want to get strange notebooks out to amaze everybody...

209 PIMP MY CAR

DECORATE THE IMAGE LEFT WITH FLASHY AND EXTRAVAGANT ACCESSORIES. Pastime fantasy game, especially suited for children.

Sawtooth tires, a rectangular steering wheel, a frontal jackhammer, an anchor, an alien in the back seat, a castle on top defended by Knights Templar, a missile launcher, machine guns, a dead body in the trunk, anti-shark powder, the rotor of a helicopter, a defect Invisibility Force Field (I.F.F.), a banana ejection propulsion jet, flame thrower, a hatch door, a cat flap, a weather balloon, a telescope, campfire with barbecue and sausages...

210 WORD FILL

LANGUAGE GAME. Put random points on a blank piece of paper. But separate each series of points. Here: 2, 4, 5...

Then try to fill it with words making a more or less rational and coherent sentence.

In the example: "WE WANT NEVER EVER GO TO NEW YORK WHEN SNOW WAS THERE."

I'm sure a better one could be found!

The two grids with handwritten digits:

Left grid:
```
        1  11 1111
    1 [ 0  1  1  1 ] 11
    1 [ 1  1  1  1 ] 111
   11 [ 1  1  0  1 ] 1
  111 [ 1  1  1  1 ] 1
        111  1  1
             11
```

Right grid:
```
        111    11  11
  111 [ 1  1  1  1 ] 1
    1 [ 1  1  1  1 ] 1+11
    1 [ 1  1  1  1 ] 1+11
  1+1 [ 1  0  0  1 ]
        1  111  1  1
                   1
```

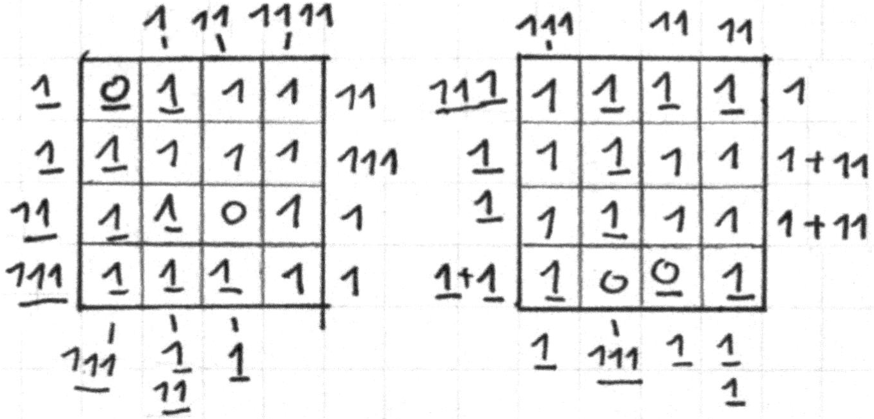

WE PLAY ON A 4 X 4 GRID. In turn, Blue and Red (here "Red" is represented by underlined numbers) place each time a digit 1.

However, they are obliged to put a zero somewhere ONCE ONLY. The goal is to reach the highest sum. That is counted horizontally AND vertically. The strategy must be to prevent your opponent to reach a high sum.

How to count: see the example. In the first field, it's clear that "not underlined" wins, since he reaches more than a thousand.

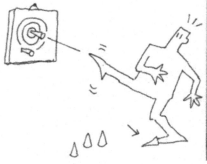

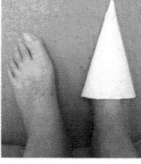

DEXTERITY GAME. Roll up light cardboard into open cones.

Maybe glue a needle in the top, as long as you can play safely.

213 PAPER CHAIN PUZZLE

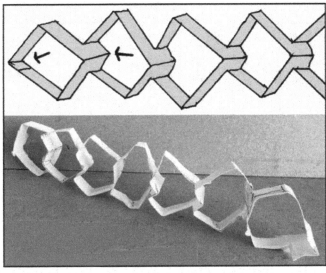

CAN YOU MAKE THE TEMPLATE FOR THIS OBJECT?

It should be in ONE piece. Flaps must of course be provided (see arrows).

This is a really difficult one. But possible. See the trial below.

214 WALK OF DEATH

0	X	0	0	X
X	X	X	X	
X	0	X	0	0
0	X	0	X	0
X	0	0	X	0

WE PLAY ON A 5 BY 5 GRID. In turn, each player places two of his marks in the field, wherever he wants. Finally, one field will be left open. That is the Afterlife.

From there on, players must draw a line of five squares long, only straight, not diagonal. See example. All these marks are dead. You may have to destroy your own marks too, since you are obliged to draw such a line. The two lines may cross each other, but not double. The second player has a certain advantage since he/she can decide where the Afterlife will fall. So the first player should draw the first Walk of Death.

In this example, it is clear that X has lost.

215 ISLAND CONNECTIONS

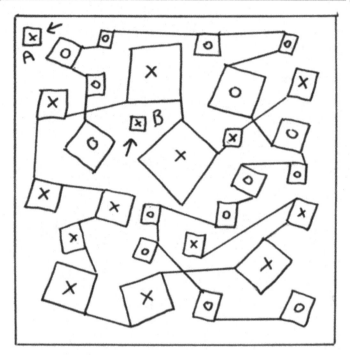

FIRST, WE DRAW A BIG SQUARE ON PAPER. Then each opponent draws, in turns, 15 squares or "islands." We draw this by hand, but the four corners must be clearly defined, and your squares may not be too small.

Then, players try to connect all of their squares with a straight line. For this, a ruler must be used. You connect from the corner of the squares. No more than TWO lines may depart from one square. You try to connect all of your islands with one continuous line. If no one succeeds, the longest connection counts.

In this example, O succeeded. But X missed two islands. It is, surprisingly, nearly always possible to make a connection, but it's more difficult to "see" the continuous line. Therefore "tryouts" are forbidden.

You must draw the lines with the ruler without hesitation. In this example, the two islands, forgotten by X could have well been connected correctly, and included in the continuous line. See B for instance, between the two bigger squares. But, unfortunately, these already have two departing lines, and more is forbidden.

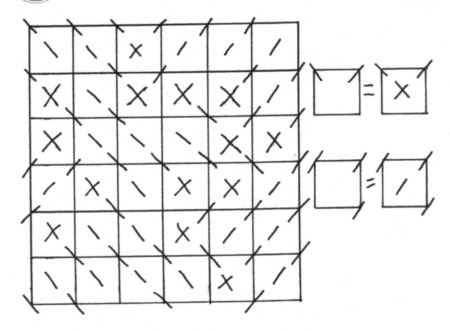

A BIT OF AN ORIGINAL GAME, since the two players don't play against each other but against an invisible third party. In fact, the two players need to cooperate.

See example: this is the board. One player uses a slash to the left, the other to the right. In turns, they mark or "occupy" a crossing point. When 3 marks at any corner of a box go to the left or right, that mark may put a slanting stripe in the middle.

If however two stripes in the corners go in opposite directions, a Cross is put in the middle. Once a slash or an X is put in the middle, it stays like this. Playing is obligatory until all the squares have a mark in the middle.

The two players are playing against the mysterious X. When X reaches more than 10, X wins. In the example, X reaches even 14.

217 POLYHEDRON FINDER

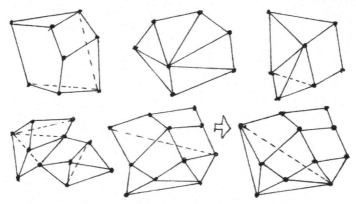

PASTIME PUZZLE. Imagine making a spatial polyhedron with a given set of random points. Will it always be possible?

First draw some points. Then try to turn them into a real object. Imagine seeing it from above: number 2 is clearly some kind of pyramid with the middle point on top. I don't know if number 4 really can exist.

The only way to find out is to make a real paper model.

218 DROODLE DOODLES

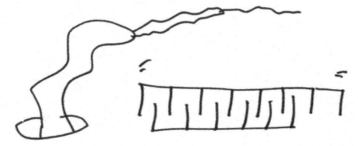

INSPIRED BY ROGER PRICE, who wrote his fantastic book DROODLES in 1953. Thus inventing a new word, a new visual style, and a new form of humor.

But today we can still try to invent new ones… Here are two of mine…
1. "Snake eating a worm eating spaghetti." 2. "Spider eating an insect."

219 ART KNOTS

ART AND PASTIME GAME. Find some bits and pieces of different string. From anywhere, preferably in different colors. Then make complicated "knots" in them. Keep the tangle open. It's...ART.

220 PICTURE LANGUAGE

PASTIME GAME. Come up with a creative and imaginative sentence. Then try to translate it into drawings. The other players must guess what is going on from the picture. "I saw two lions chasing a buffalo, but one lion fell into the river, and was eaten by a crocodile, while the other lion stepped on a landmine."

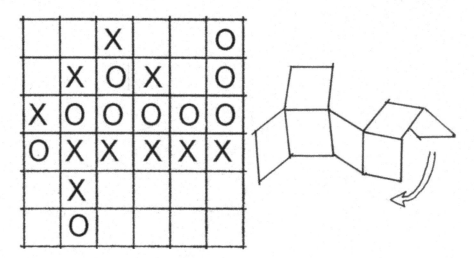

A MUCH SIMPLER VARIATION OF ANOTHER GAME IN THIS BOOK: CUBE UNFOLDER.

We play on a grid 6 x 6. In turn, players put down their mark, here O and X. The first one who can make a "Cube" wins.

O can make one, see the drawing (double sides to reach the bottom or the roof are allowed). And since X started, the turns are equal.

If the board is made larger there are more chances to find a cube. If it's a draw, the player who needed the least amount of squares to construct his cube wins.

CROSS CORNERS

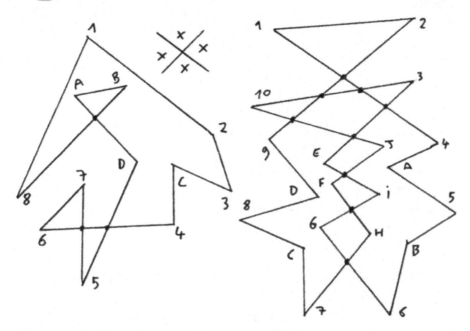

SEE THE FIRST DRAWING. Try to draw a figure with corners that point inwards or outwards. An "inward" corner points towards the INSIDE of the closed figure, or is SITUATED IN the closed figure. For example A and B.

Another rule is: a cross is created by 3 or more lines coming together in one point. Here the inwards pointing corners do NOT count. See drawing.

So, for the first drawing, we got: 8 outside corners, 4 inside, plus 3 crosses.

Now can we design a figure with an EQUAL NUMBER of inside and outside corners, plus crosses? See second example: 10 out, 10 in, and 9 crosses.

A creditable effort.

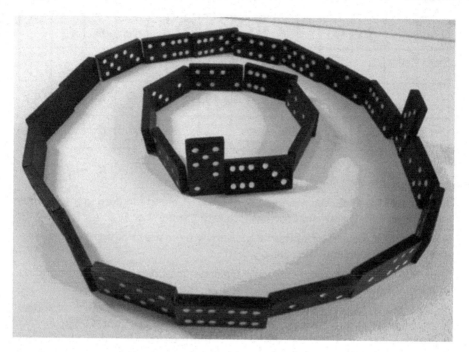

A DEXTERITY GAME that is also a (big) challenge for your intuition.

Take a dominoes set, and try to build a full circle with a small one inside. The stones MUST touch each other.

If needed, you are allowed to close the last gap with a stone that has been set upright.

The goal is to make both circles in ONE try.

NUMBER EXPLOSION

7	6	5	4
8	1	3	②
⑧	2	①	③
⑦	⑥	⑤	④

12 – ⑮

6	⑤	④	⑦
5	1	⑥	③
4	2	①	②
	3		

9 – ③

10	11	12	①
9	1	2	②
8	7	3	③
6	5	4	④

45 – ⓪

A VERY FAST GAME. We play on a 4 x 4 grid. Blue and red (Red in the example is the circled digit) each start somewhere with the number 1.

From there on they count further. A move may be made straight or diagonally. Both players go on until they are blocked.

Then the highest numbers "explode." Doing so they destroy the 8 surrounding squares. Whoever has left the highest sum on the board, wins.

EXAMPLES. A. Both players managed to reach the number 8. Both 8 explode. B. 6 is blocked in the upper left corner. And Circle 7 at the right. C. Circle numbers only reach 4. "Blue" reaches 12. After the explosion of 12 and Circle 4, "Blue" gets 45 points.

225 STRAIGHT LINES DRAWINGS

HERE AGAIN ARE SOME IDEAS FOR DRAWINGS made up of only straight lines. It's of course much easier to draw like that. Nevertheless, a surprising result can be achieved, certainly when you color it. Plus it's a good exercise in learning how to draw.

226 DOMINO FILL

TAKE A SET OF DOMINOES, guess how big the surface will be if you lay them together in an orderly fashion, and then use half of that area (or less).

Draw this board on paper. Now players may, in turns, lay 1 domino flat in this field until no player can do that without touching another domino, which is strictly forbidden. That player loses 1 point. But then he is allowed to put the dominoes on their narrow side.

Again, this is permissible until 1 player can't place his domino this way. She loses 1 point. But then she is allowed to put dominoes on their head. This way they take even less space. And then, finally, the player who has no place left for this, loses 1 point.

So, it's possible to win the first two rounds, but lose the third, and still be the winner. It could be handy to have two sets of dominoes at hand. Or combine them with other objects.

227 THE A LANGUAGE

"WE SAT AROUND THE TABLE and discussed the replacement of all the vowels by the A in the English language

"Wa sat araand tha tabla and dascassad tha raplacamant af all tha vawals ba tha A an tha Anglash langaaga."

Improvise!

A FAST AND SIMPLE VARIATION ON TCHUKA RUMA, a solitaire Mancala game. Each player has his own pit or "Ruma": R1 and R2. You have to imagine that you play with pebbles. See the drawing for the starting situation.

There are 8 pebbles, ordered like this. R1 plays clockwise, R2 counterclockwise. You may start from any "pit" (except the Ruma's), and distribute -"sow"- ALL the little pebbles in there to the other pits. Only 1 per pit.

In the example, R1 started (see arrow). He took 2 out of the first pit and distributed them clockwise. He then drew the new situation on the board. Then R2 plays, see arrow, and the result is visible in row 3. And so on.

If you have too many pebbles, you go further on the other side. So on in a circle. You lose if your last pebble falls in an empty pit (except the Ruma).

The goal is to collect as many pebbles as possible in your Ruma. In the example (row 5) R1 is lost. Whether he sows from the pit with 1 pebble or the one with 6, he will always end in an empty pit.

ROW ROW

A	B	C	D	E	F	G	H	i	J
1	1	1	1	1	1	1	1	1	1
0	1	2	1	1	1	1	1	1	1
0	1	2	1	1	1	1	2	1	0
0	0	2	2	1	1	1	2	1	0
0	0	2	2	1	1	2	2	0	0

A	B	C	D	E	F	G	H	i	J
1	1	1	1	1	1	1	1	1	1
0	1	1	2	1	1	1	1	1	1
0	1	1	2	1	1	2	1	1	0
0	0	1	2	2	1	2	1	1	0
0	0	1	2	2	0	2	1	2	0
0	0	0	2	2	1	2	1	2	0
0	0	0	2	2	2	2	0	2	0

QUARREL IN A ROW! IMAGINE A ROW OF 10 COINS. These coins are allowed to jump over 1 other coin. So 1 coin becomes 2.

The goal is to form a row of 2 coins each. See the first diagram. A jumps over B, J over I, and I over H. And now we are blocked. Is it possible to find a solution?

Now look at the second diagram. Here we are allowed to jump over 1, but also over 2 other coins. So the A jumps over B AND C. And so on. Now we end up with all 2's. But…not next to each other. So explore this game further.

Try it with other numbers. Try 9 or 15 (rows of 3)…

ONE TO TEN SENTENCES

TRY TO CONSTRUCT A SMALL STORY where you use the numbers one to ten. They don't have to be in numerical order.

"In the park, TWO men saw THREE girls, walking on SIX sneakers, with FOUR dogs. 'Hey', said the men, 'together we are FIVE people. Why don't we move our TEN feet, and go eat a waffle at The Belgian, it's open EIGHT days a week.' 'But together we are NINE', laughed the girls, 'when you include our dogs. Anyway there are only SEVEN days in ONE week, you idiots'.

6	9	6	21	10	1	10		8	8	7
9	60	9	⇨	1	44	1		11	62	5
6	9	6	21	10	1	10		4	8	11

21   21

PUZZLE GAME. WE DRAW A 3 X 3 GRID. We write 8 digits along the side rows/columns, leaving the middle square open. However, the sum of those individual rows and columns must be 21: see example. The total sum is 60.

Now try to diminish that sum of 60, but by keeping the sum of the rows and columns 21. See the second example. This is the limit: the sum is now 44. Find all the variations in between.

The same for the third example. Here the sums are 23. And the total is 62. You are allowed to go over 10 and use zero.

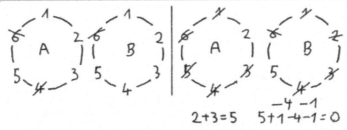

$$2+3=5 \qquad 5+1-4-1=0$$

A GAME OF CHANCE. Each opponent writes the digits 1 to 6 in a circle.

Next, they throw a dice in turns. See example. If A throws a 6, he may cross out the 6 of his opponent B. However, when A throws another 6, he has to destroy his own 6. And when someone has a third 6, he gets a penalty of MINUS 6. A throw: 6 - 6 - 3 - 2 - 1- 3 (you only get 6 turns). And B: 4 - 5 - 1 - 4 - 4 - 1. Plus B got the penalty points: minus 4 and 1.

The final score consists of the digits you leave in the circle, plus the LAST score of your dice, minus your penalty points. A gets 2 + 3 (last throw of his dice) = 5. And B: 5 + 1 – 4 – 1= 1.

Not a "Brain Game"? Yes, but INVENTING all kinds of variations of Dice or Domino Games is. So, invent a few new ones…

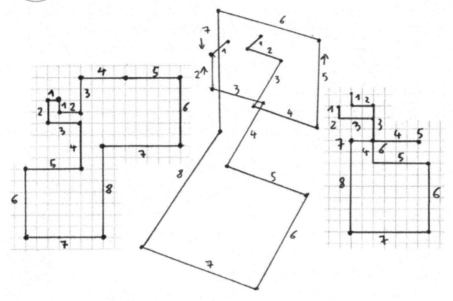

ON SQUARED PAPER, draw lines going from 1 square wide to 8, and then back again, from 8 to 1, trying to close the figure. See the example on the left. We are not obliged to change direction every time. Now this is rather easy. Although the fun is to achieve this "intuitively." But when we must include the third dimension, it can become more difficult. See example in the middle.

Line 5 goes UP, 6 is flat again, 7 goes DOWN, and 2 goes UP again. Now I made only one attempt at this, but it failed.

The last 1 is on the right height, but misses 1 in the length and 1 in the width (but if the origin point 1 was in the extension of line 2, it would have succeeded). But on the right, we see that we can easily translate the third dimension on a flat surface.

You see: point 5 goes UP, 6 is above 4, 7 goes down, and point 2 goes up again. If we keep track of the heights, we can draw very complex "wire structures" in space.

Try to go to 20 and back, on several levels of height.

234 MAZE TRACE

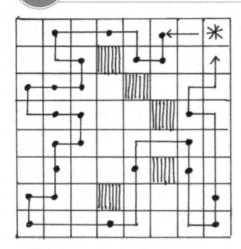

EACH PLAYER DRAWS AN 8 X 8 GRID. In each row each player places 3 dots, wherever he wants.

In addition players may draw 5 "blocks", but without closing off a part of the field.

Next, players give each other their design. Then start in the square top right, and try to connect all the dots. Only straight moves allowed.

Do not visit the same dot twice, or repeat an existing line.

235 MAD ADD MATH

SOLO PUZZLE GAME. We write two times the row of digits 1 to 10. Then we add two digits up. Those two plus their sum are crossed out. See the example on top. 5 + 5 = 10. 6 + 3 = 9. 6 + 3 = 9. 2 + 8 = 10. 1 + 7 = 8. All these digits are destroyed. The rest is underlined, and their sum is 18. No other sums are possible.

The goal is to reach the lowest possible total sum that is left. In example 2 we do better. The total sum of the untouched digits is 10. And in the bottom row only 6.

Can we go lower?

FINGER FIST

A

B

ADAPTATION ON PAPER OF AN OLD GAME played with two hands.

Imagine two opponents facing each other, able to stick up fingers. See first row: they start with one finger (stripe) up on each hand. For each move, they can add two sides up (tapping), and add left to right or vice versa, or do nothing (free choice).

Or they can directly transfer the left or the right to one "hand" of the opponent (obligatory). Sounds complicated, but look at the example.

The arrow outside indicates the player in action. So B adds one stripe to the left, becoming 2. That player then gives that 2 to A left, becoming three. (If you go OVER 5, for instance, 4 + 2 = 6, then you have to SUBTRACT 5. So you get 1. See the second row.)

The winner is the one who can reach 5 (a "closed fist", here Zero). Examples: each row is 1 move. Two columns, two games. The drawings make it more clear than the text.

237 SQUARE TOWER

IMAGINE YOU HAVE 8 EQUAL CARDBOARD SQUARES.

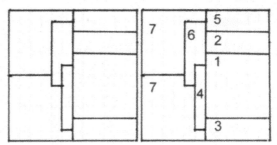

Now lay them on top of each other, so that always a part of the underlying square is still visible. See the first drawing.

Now give this to your opponent and ask him/her to number the layers. The one on top is number 1. See the solution in the second drawing (2 is on 3, but that could be reversed).

Finally, we reach two squares level 7. Use squared paper.

Make the first design in pencil, and each time you lay another square on top, erase the covered lines.

Then redraw the final result in pen (otherwise your opponent will see the erased pencil lines).

You can also make the squares bigger, and use 10 squares. This has the potential to become a very complicated puzzle.

238 CASTLE KEYS

THIS KIND OF PUZZLE DOES OF COURSE ALREADY EXIST.

But here we present it as a game.

First, draw a "castle" and make a maze. Now insert several "doors" and try to make it as complicated as possible. Then draw the map again, but without the solution, and give it to your opponent. However, you will find out that creating a maze is more complicated than solving it. So, it's two puzzles in one.

Try to invent a nearly unsolvable one. Now the problem is: a valet has to lock all the doors. How does he do that without going through the

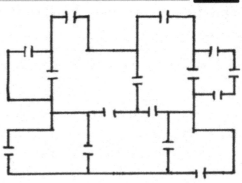

same door twice? Many variations are possible.

For instance: it's raining outside, and the valet wants to stay inside. Which is the least number of doors he'll have to pass twice?

DIAGOLINE

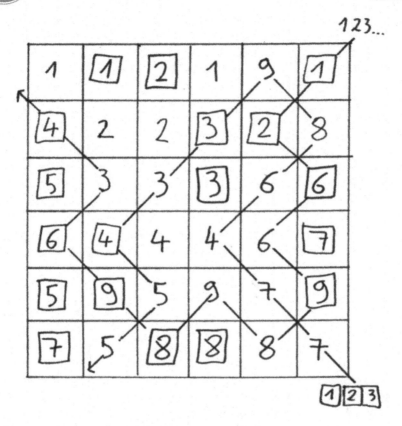

ON A 6 X 6 GRID, PLAYERS WRITE THE DIGITS 1 TO 9, and then again 1 to 9 on the field. This is in turn, and in different colors.

After that, each may draw ONE CONTINUOUS line on the board, that line must ALWAYS run diagonally. The goal is to destroy as many enemy digits as possible, although you'll probably have to destroy some of your own.

It is forbidden to follow the same line twice or go through already destroyed digits. See example: normal digits and outlined ones.

A bit confusing without the use of colors of course. Outlined is left with 1,2,5,3,7,5,7,8. And blank ones only with 1,1,2,2,4.